Provence

From The Course Study Tours (with Langascons)
1 - 3 May 2005.

Not particularly helpful.

GW00373931

Discovery CHANNEL

APA PUBLICATIONS L
Part of the Langenscheidt Publishing Group

Welcome!

T his guidebook combines the interests and enthusi-
asms of two of the world's best-known information
providers: Insight Guides, who have set the standard
for visual travel guides since 1970, and Discovery
Channel, the world's premier source of nonfiction tele-
vision programming. It aims to bring you the best of
Provence in tailor-made itineraries devised by Insight's
correspondent, Mark Fincham.

The guide begins at the foot of Mt-Ventoux with a
tour around the Dentelles de Montmirail. It then heads
south to Avignon, an ancient Rhône staging post and
erstwhile home to the popes, from where it is a short
hop to Arles. From there you can head to sophisticated
Aix-en-Provence and then to the coast, to Cassis, the
Ile de Porquerolles and St-Tropez. Our correspondent
then turns inland again to explore the Var and the
Luberon. The guide also includes an introduction to the
history of the area, plus a section packed with practical tips and restaurant and hotel recommendations.

Mark Fincham first went to live in Provence
in the summer of 1982, when he enjoyed
long hot days of idleness and pleasure. At
the time he did not think he had been
especially smitten, but when summer came round again
he thought only of Provence. Then he found himself
arriving for the *réveillon*, the celebration of the New
Year when the skies are blown clear by the mistral.
Soon he was coming for Easter and then for the
vendange (grape harvest). Finally he bowed to the in-
evitable and moved to the region.

C O N T E N T S

Pages 2/3: Roussillon in the Luberon

Pages 8/9: the harbour at Cassis

HISTORY

In his book on Provence, Ford Madox Ford described the region as 'a highway along which travelled continuously the stream of the arts, of thought, of the traditions of life'. The process he so aptly describes has created what could be identified as the supreme type of Mediterranean culture. The presiding genius is, of course, that great gift, the sun. Its characteristic features are the products of the olive and grape, the universal cafés, the *cours* and *boulevards* where people meet and talk, the customary evening promenade, an *apéritif* and a game of *boules*, the love of running water expressed in the ubiquitous fountains, the many social and cultural manifestations such as village fêtes, markets, concerts and theatre and, in winter, the devotion to *la chasse* (the hunt). In this brief history I hope to show how all this came about.

The Greeks first introduced the vine

The Greeks

The Greeks who came to Provence in 600BC are attributed with introducing the techniques for cultivating vines. Today vineyards cover 40,000 hectares (155 sq. miles) of land, or nearly half the region. They are the chief characteristic of the Provençal country-side, and their wines are found on every table. The other gift of the Greeks was the olive tree. Though less extensive than the vine, it has nevertheless contributed to another of the definitive characteristics of Provençal culture – a cuisine based on olive oil (as opposed to butter).

The overriding dominance of the vine in the Provençal country-side has been steadily reduced over the last 50 years, as irrigation schemes have enabled intensive cultivation of fruits and vegetables less suited to dry conditions. These schemes include the taming of the Durance and Verdon rivers by building dams at Serre-Ponçon and Saint-Croix, and the creation of Le Canal de Provence which feeds a 3,000-km (1,850-mile) system of irrigation canals. The intensive cultivation of peaches, apples and sunflowers that are such a distinctive feature of the Vaucluse and Bouches-de-Rhône regions was unknown 25 years ago. Today Provence accounts for 35 percent of national production of vegetables and 25 percent of fruits.

The Romans

The Romans founded their first settlement in Provence in 122BC after their victory over the indigenous tribes, variously described as Franks or Gauls. The site, named Aquae Sextiae, would eventually become Aix-en-Provence. This was the beginning of Roman rule in Provence and it lasted until the fall of the Roman Empire in AD476. Curiously, the Romans had originally come to Provence to

Roman ruins at St Remy

help their traditional allies, the Greeks, whose trading ambitions were hindered by the Gauls. However, they increasingly began to see Provence as a stepping-stone between Italy and Spain, the spoil of their victory over the Carthaginians. They also liked what they found and named it *Provincia* – the Roman province. In 103BC the Roman general Marius consolidated Rome's hold on the area by defeating a huge army of Teutons from northern Europe. The name Marius has lived on in the common memory and until recently was a common boy's name in Provence.

Unlike the Greeks, who came to Provence to trade, the Romans were true imperialists. The whole cultural apparatus of Rome was imposed on the new province. Towns were built according to the Roman urban plan and each one had its own individual forum, arena, theatre, public baths and fountains, and three great roads were constructed to link them – the Aurelian Way, the Agrippan Way and the Domitian Way.

Vestiges of this titanic building programme can be seen all over Provence, in small bridges and ruins and often in antique remains incorporated into the walls of contemporary buildings, as in the Nord-Pinus Hotel in Arles. Then there are the mighty public buildings of Fréjus, Arles, Nîmes, Orange and Vaison. This heritage has profoundly influenced the shape of present-day Provence. The central *cours* or *place* and the fountain of every town and village are derived from the Roman forum. In Aix-en-Provence these fountains are the Roman signature on a town that at first sight bears little imprint of its Roman history, since they are animated by the thermal springs, the *aquae* after which Sextius named this site.

The great Roman arenas of Fréjus, Arles, Nîmes and Orange are a graphic illustration of the way in which Provence has absorbed and adapted its past. One moment they are mute witnesses to Provençal history, the next a vital part of contemporary cultural life, as venues for concerts and bullfights. At the moment when the matador is lining up for the kill and the crowd quietens in anticipation it is almost impossible to imagine that the arena ever existed for any other purpose.

The Christians

Christianity, no less than the Greeks or the Romans, left its imprint on the complex grid of Provençal history. From the legendary conversion of Provence to Christianity in the 1st century,

Early representations of Christ

after the miraculous landing of the boat from Judea – the so-called Boat of Bethany – bearing amongst others, Lazarus, Mary Magdalene and Martha, religion has exerted a strong influence.

Monasticism took an early hold and in the 12th century the Cistercians built the great Romanesque abbeys of Sénanque, Silvacane and Thoronet. Perhaps not surprisingly the heavy, simple forms of the Romanesque – with their reminder of classical shapes – struck a chord in Provence, unleashing an intense period of building activity. Romanesque churches from this period are a distinctive feature of many Provençal villages.

Provence was also a destination for pilgrims who came to the superb Gothic basilica of St Maximin, which stands on the spot where, according to legend, Mary Magdalene was buried. The papacy came to Avignon in the 14th century putting Provence, for a short while, at the centre of the Christian world. Though the popes returned to Rome in 1377, they retained control of an area known as the *Comtat Venaissin* (today the department of the Vaucluse) and their influence and the magnificent legacy of their building continued to inform the life of this area, notably in the Religious Wars of the 16th century when many Protestant villages in the Luberon were destroyed.

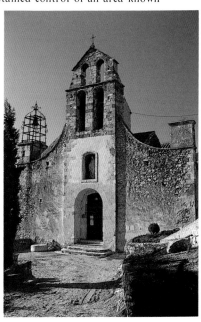

Though religious observance has declined, the Christian history of Provence still influences the *fêtes* that are part of the cultural life of every village. Some are clearly part of the Christian tradition, such as the *fêtes* of the Nativity on Christmas Eve, when the Nativity is enacted by members of the village (one of the best known of these is in the village of Séguret in the Vaucluse). This is itself an extension of the popular Provençal custom of deco-

The Romanesque church at Gigondas

rating a crib with *santons* – clay figures representing the cast of the Nativity. Collections of these figures are found in all the regional museums devoted to popular culture and are considered typically Provençal. However, this practice was actually imported from Italy in the 16th century and rapidly incorporated into Provençal culture.

'Houses in Provence' by Cézanne, who was born in Aix-en-Provence

In many cases the Christian foundations of a *fête* have been forgotten or overlayed with a new meaning and the *fête* has become a popular celebration. One such is the rowdy *Bravade* of 16 May in St-Tropez celebrating the naming of the town after the Roman martyr Torpes (Tropez), who was decapitated after converting to Christianity and washed up in the one-time fishing port that now bears his name. More famous is the *Fête et pélerinage* to Les-Saintes-Maries-de-la-Mer. The 700-year-old annual pilgrimage to the town where the Boat of Bethany landed is now famous as a two-day festival of the gypsies. Their patron saint is Sarah, the slave of the Marys (Magdalene, Salomé and Jacobé) who arrived in the boat.

A New Breed of Visitor

In 1763 the English writer Tobias Smollett travelled to the South of France in search of a climate that might restore his health. Although Smollett did not find his trip an agreeable experience, the published account of his travels brought the climate of the south, particularly the crisp, dry winters, to the attention of a larger public. He wrote, 'There is less rain and wind at Nice than in any other part of the world that I know... [the] air being dry, pure, heavy, and elastic, must be agreeable to the constitution of those who labour under disorders, arising from weak nerves, obstructed perspiration... a viscidity of lymph, and a languid circulation.' Since this described a broad variety of disorders Smollett was soon followed by coach-loads of invalids, and also by the English aristocracy, who took to wintering on the Riviera to escape the damp and cold of England.

For these first tourists the season lasted only from November to March. The summer was considered hot and unhealthy until the 1920s, when a few daring Americans persuaded one hotel owner to remain open in the summer.

The French were generally less excited by the discovery of the South of France, though they established resorts in Hyères and St-Raphael. The introduction of the paid holiday in 1936 – two weeks statutory minimum – changed all that, and they too began flocking to the south, many of them in order to see the sea for the first time.

A parallel development was a migration of artists and writers to the South of France. The artists were attracted by the clarity of the Mediterranean light and the writers drawn by the cheap living conditions. The first artists whose work publicised the area and shaped people's perceptions of it were the painters Vincent Van Gogh, Paul Cézanne and Paul Signac. A number of writers were also influential, including Colette, F. Scott Fitzgerald, Somerset Maugham and Françoise Sagan, who all published books set in Provence. They contributed to a rising tide of publicity that created the image of a warm Mediterranean paradise and helped establish the reputation of Provence as the place for those interested in the arts.

All this publicity was as nothing compared to the tumult that was unleashed by one *artiste* at the end of the 1950s. Her name was Brigitte Bardot and the scenes of her making love and swimming naked at St-Tropez in the film *And God Created Woman*, brought St-Tropez and Provence to the notice of the world, and brought the world to St-Tropez and Provence.

Year-round sun brought tourism

By the year 2000 the number of visitors to Provence had risen to 25 million, attracted by the myth fostered by Brigitte Bardot, the opportunities for leisure offered by a climate averaging 2,800 hours of sunshine per annum and the rich cultural environment. Today tourism is the primary industry in Provence.

The Provençals

What are the people like who preside over all this? Since antiquity Provence has lain on one of the great highways of Europe and the region has consequently assimilated many different peoples of the Mediterranean. In the Arles region, the influence of Spain can be seen in the people and their local customs, most obviously in the bullfight; the last major influx of Spaniards were refugees from the Spanish Civil War. In the coastal region around Marseilles the people are still said to bear the imprint of their Greek heritage. And in the Var and the area surrounding Nice the influence of Italy can be clearly seen. Nice was an Italian possession for centuries and received, along with the Var, a large influx of Italians at the end of the 19th century. Since 1950 the south of France has received many settlers from Algeria, Tunisia and Morocco. They have been accommodated less smoothly than the Mediterranean races but their influence is certainly reflected, for example, in the cuisine of this part of Provence.

These influxes have made for an open society, where the foreigner is not an object of suspicion. Provençals are generally welcoming and they enjoy contact with other people, particularly if this leads to a large general discussion. Their philosophy is live and let live. Paradoxically, however, this does not always extend to their own countrymen.

This attitude can be traced deep in the history of Provence, a history of separation and independence from the rest of France. Politically it was not joined to the kingdom of France until 1481. Culturally its links were with the Mediterranean countries. French did not replace Provençal as the official language of Provence until 1539. The papal court in Avignon conducted its affairs in Latin and Provençal – known as the *langue d'oc*. As Provence came increasingly under the sway of the centralising and unifying power of the state in the 19th century, a movement arose called the *Félibrige*, whose essential aim was to assert and preserve its cultural independence, including the revival of interest in the *langue d'oc*.

One of the best reasons for visiting Provence

Historical Highlights

600BC Greek traders found the port of Marseille, bringing the olive tree and the vine with them to Provence.

122 Foundation of Aquae-Sextiae (Aix-en-Provence) by the Romans.

103 The Roman general Marius defeats the Teutons.

58–51 Subjugation of Gaul by Julius Caesar. Romans impose imperial rule on their new province.

19 Building of the Pont du Gard, which still exists today.

12 Romans occupy the settlement at Vaison.

AD46 The Boat of Bethany lands at Les Saintes-Maries-de-la-Mer.

476 Fall of the Roman Empire.

500 Vaison is invaded by the Burgundians.

536 Provence comes under the rule of the Franks.

1032 Provence is annexed to the Holy Roman Empire.

1125 The flowering of Troubador poetry and the Courts of Love, exemplified in Les Baux.

1152 Consecration of the church of St-Trophime.

1160 Foundation of the abbey of Sénanque.

1309 Clement V, a Frenchman, is given the papal crown.

1316 Pope John XXII establishes the papacy in Avignon.

1388 The eastern part of Provence, known as the County of Nice, comes under the rule of the House of Savoy (Italy).

1409 University of Aix is founded.

1481 Provence is joined to the kingdom of France.

1539 French replaces Provençal, the *langue d'oc*, as the official language.

1545 Destruction of Protestant villages in the Luberon during the Wars of Religion.

1763 English writer Tobias Smollett travels through the South of France; his writing attracted the first tourists – even though it wasn't entirely complimentary.

1789 The French Revolution.

1790 Provence is divided into three *départements*: Basse-Alpes, Bouches-du-Rhône and Var.

1815 The end of the Napoleonic Wars, the English aristocracy begins to winter in the south of France.

1839 Cézanne is born in Aix.

1854 Founding of the *Félibrige*.

1855 Paris–Avignon railway built.

1860 The County of Nice is returned to France.

1865 Nice is linked by rail to Marseille and the valley of the Rhône.

1869 Publication of Daudet's *Lettres de Mon Moulin*.

1887 The term Côte d'Azur is coined.

1888 Van Gogh settles in Arles.

1892 The pontillist painter, Paul Signac, settles in St-Tropez.

1923 Regulations for the production of wines in Châteauneuf-du-Pape are introduced.

1925 The writer Colette moves to St Tropez.

1936 Introduction of the paid holiday in France.

1941 Bandol receives *appellation contrôlée* status.

1944 The Allies land on the beaches of Pampelonne towards the end of World War II.

1956 Foundation of *La Société du Canal de Provence*.

1960 Serre-Ponçon dam opens.

1960 Brigitte Bardot hits St-Tropez, starring in the film *And God Created Woman*.

1970 A6–A7 motorway, the *autoroute du soleil*, links Paris and the South.

1975 The Sainte-Croix dam opens.

1976 Completion of *Le Canal de Provence*.

1981 The TGV (*Train à Grand Vitesse*) links Paris and Nice.

1992 Treaty of Maastricht attempts to unify Europe.

1992 Catastrophic flooding in Provence.

1998 The Front National attracts 27 percent of votes in the region.

2001 The Paris to Marseille TGV link opens.

Provence

25 miles / 40 km

Day Itiner

The southeast corner of France is known as Provence-Alpes-Côte d'Azur and is divided into six *départements*, Alpes-de-Haute-Provence, Hautes-Alpes, Alpes-Maritimes, Bouches-du-Rhône, Var and Vaucluse. However, the boundaries of the 'real' Provence, like the ingredients of the 'real' *bouillabaisse*, are a subject of dispute.

The area covered by this guide is contained within the *départements* of the Vaucluse, Bouches-du-Rhône and Var. A car is highly recommended for these itineraries, although any one of them could be achieved in a day by a good touring cyclist. The routes describe an uneven circle, starting in the north at the foot of Mt-Ventoux, heading south towards the coast, moving along the coast, then heading inland and finally back west towards Mt-Ventoux. Places to stay are recommended in the *Practical Information* section, with a price guide.

Most of the tours would benefit from starting before 9.30am, before the day really has a chance to warm up. The tours are also shaped by the desirability of eating at lunchtime. I say this not only because this will be a good time to stop and absorb the morning's sights, but because in France the main meal is often at noon (usually covering two hours, from noon until 2pm). This is also the best time to find the local speciality on the 80FF lunch menu.

Preceding pages: Provence has a long tradition of artists. Below: ready to go

Suggestions as to what to do during between 2pm and 5pm, when the sun can really burn, are also provided. As the ideal solution – taking a siesta – is not always an option, I have tried to ensure that by this time of the day the itinerary will take you either into the countryside, where there should be shade, or near water. A range of places to stay is included in the *Accommodation* section beginning on page 84.

The Dentelles de Montmirail

The Vaucluse

1. Picturesque Provence

A circuit of the Dentelles de Montmirail, taking in Roman ruins, medieval towns, perched villages, 'santons', the sumptuous fruity wines of Gigondas and the decadent sweet wines of Beaumes-de-Venise. 63 km (39 miles).

The **Dentelles de Montmirail** is a chain of mountains extending over about 15km (9 miles) of the **Vaucluse**, a *département* of great natural beauty known in France for the quality of its fresh fruit and vegetables. I would recommend **Bédoin,** nestling in the sunny pastures at the foot of the Mt-Ventoux, as an ideal base. Begin the day at the *Office du Tourisme*, where the *accueil* (welcome) is always warm and they are generous with local maps and guides.

The D19 from Bédoin to **Malaucène** snakes between the Dentelles and the lower slopes of Mt-Ventoux, with soaring mountain scenery opening out on all sides. The fortress-like south front of the parish church of St-Michael greets you as you enter Malaucène; in summer the people of the town like to sit on the cool stone bench at the base of this wall. As the gateway to the Alpine north face of the Mt-Ventoux, Malaucène is a busy town, but time can be better spent at our main morning destination, **Vaison-la-Romaine**.

The D938 leaves Malaucène in the shade of a long avenue of trees and before long the medieval quarter of Vaison comes into view,

The fortified medieval village of Vaison-la-Romaine

hanging precariously over the road. Cross the Roman bridge that was seriously damaged by floods in 1992 but has since been restored, and leave your car in the large space in the town centre. From here Vaison is easily explored on foot.

The town splits into two distinct parts, separated by the River Ouvèze. On one side are the Roman and present-day towns, on the other the medieval town and traces of an earlier Celtic occupation. The main Roman site known as the **Quartier de Puymin** (entrance opposite the Tourist Office) with a museum, ancient theatre and large villa is magnificent and should not be missed. It is in my view far more impressive than the celebrated Roman site at Glanum just outside St-Rémy. Contemporary accounts described it as the *urbs opulentissima* and one can imagine this was justified. One ticket gives admission to the Roman ruins, the on-site museum and the cloisters of the town's cathedral, **Notre-Dame-de-Nazareth**. The opening times are the same for all sites (closed Tuesday). For further information, call the tourist office on 04 9036 0211.

A five-minute walk down the Grand Rue and back across the Roman bridge brings you to the heavily fortified medieval village surmounted by its ruined castle. The maze of streets contains a number of craft shops and an interesting 17th-century hotel. The lanes are rewarding to explore, but first turn left past the fountain under the Porte Vielle-Rue de l'Horloge and follow Rue d'Eglise past a fine row of cottages until you come to Le Planet, from where there is an excellent view. From here Rue de Charité leads up to the ruined castle.

Back in the main town Place Montfort – swamped by a market on Tuesday – is lined by *brasseries* on one side and is a good place to have a beer or perhaps a cup of tea at **Café des Arts**, an old-fashioned café

Well-proportioned Roman, Vaison

on the corner of the square below the Hôtel des Lis. Afterwards, for all but the most ardent fan of Roman history, it is probably time to leave Vaison.

The next place on this itinerary is **Séguret**. Leave Vaison on the D977 (direction Carpentras) and after 5km (3 miles) turn off onto the D88 (direction Séguret). The exits from Vaison are not entirely clear and if you find yourself on the D975, direction Orange, don't worry – continue to Roaix, take the D7 on your left, which crosses the River Ouvèze, and go straight across the D977 onto the D88 to Séguret. This is what the French call a *route du vin*, literally a wine-road, and you will see on all sides the vines belonging to the area designated Côte du Rhône Villages, of which Séguret is one.

As a general rule, the wines from these villages will be of a higher quality than a wine that is designated simply Côte du Rhône.

Séguret has two superb restaurants, **Le Mesclun** *(see page 73)* and **La Table du Comtat** *(see page 84)*, and it is difficult to choose between them. La Table du Comtat is also a small hotel and is therefore smarter and more expensive; the owner-chef is a member of the exclusive order *Maître Cuisinier de France* and his cooking has a high reputation. Le Mesclun

Seasonal produce is his business

is a different type of establishment; each day they propose a new menu taking advantage of the seasonal produce, and for 175FF you can eat one of the best meals of your life. If you arrive too late for lunch, you can find a snack at **Lou Bàrri**, a charming *salon de thé*.

Having said all this, to eat lunch is not the only reason to come to Séguret. Its aspect overlooking the Plain of Orange is glorious. The village, which is designated as a national monument, has a 12th-century church, 14th-century belfry and a superb 17th-century fountain. It is further celebrated for its Nativity play on Christmas Eve. The parts are filled by villagers and handed down through families. This is a variation on the traditional crèche peopled by symbolic clay figures called *santons*, a feature of Christmas in Provence.

These figures can all be seen in **L'Oustau Dei Santoun** of Jean-Louis Romère, near the top of the village past the Cellier des Vignerons. His atelier contains *santons* from the two greatest masters of the craft, Paul Fouque of Aix-en-Provence and Marcel Carbonel of Marseille. He will be happy to show you the different styles of *santons* and discuss their history.

Jean-Louis wears another hat as a wine-maker, and you should not leave without a bottle or two of his extraordinary red wine, made in traditional style from very old vines. It is a real *vin du garde* (a wine to keep).

Below this 'balcony' town, as it is sometimes called, you can see the town of Sablet, whose streets are built in concentric circles around the church in a fashion that is typically Provençal. Sablet has many picturesque streets and an excellent *caveau des vignerons*, where you can taste all the local wines.

The next stop is the celebrated wine town of Gigondas, a few

The wines of Beaumes-de-Venise are sweet

kilometres further down the D7. However, real wine enthusiasts should look out for a left turn about half-way between Sablet and Gigondas and the sign for Domaine les Pallières. I can never pass this sign without being drawn up the old track to the Roux brothers' dark and winey barn. Their estate is perfectly situated in the foothills of the Dentelles and makes one of the best wines of the *appellation*. The best Gigondas are dense, ruby-coloured wines loaded with fruit and alcohol, and though some producers will advise you to keep them for up to 10 years, they can be drunk immediately, an irresistible reason for buying.

Gigondas is the Vauclusian equivalent of the one-horse town: its horse is the vine, stabled in the Caveau du Gigondas in the Place

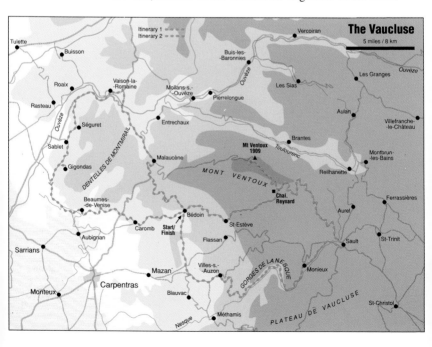

de la Marie, where you can taste and buy the wines of all the local producers. The village is dominated by its church and the vestiges of the château constructed in the 14th century by the counts of Orange. Wind your way through the old streets to the terrace of the church for another great panorama. Gigondas is a starting point for many walks in the Dentelles, and though these may have to wait for another day, you could take your car up to the orientation point of the Col du Cayron (396m/1,300ft), facing the mountain peaks.

Over the ridge is **Beaumes-de-Venise**, only a 10-minute drive by way of the D7 (direction Carpentras) and the D81, which branches off to the left after about 6km (4 miles). Sheltered from the mistral at the foot of the Durban Plateau, the town is chiefly famous for its decadently sweet wine, the Muscat de Beaumes-de-Venise. The muscat grapes grown on the super-warm south-facing slopes attain a heady degree of alcohol and seem to soak up the aromas of the apricots and peaches that load the trees in summer. This heady nectar is taken locally as an *apéritif*, a habit frowned on by purists who believe that it should be exclusively a dessert wine.

The red wines labelled Côtes du Rhône Villages also merit attention. Those I bought from the Gigondas estate of Les Goubert are some of the best wines from the Southern Rhône I have had the pleasure to drink.

Domaine Durban makes one of the best Muscats and the twisting climb up to this estate (take the D21 out of the town, turn left immediately onto route de Lafare, turn left again where you will see signs to the estate) reveals another face of the Dentelles – now steep, terraced slopes looking like the green foothills of the Andes. It is appropriate to finish the day with a glass of sweet wine in your hand and the Dentelles spread out before you.

From Beaumes-de-Venise it is a short drive back to Bédoin, via Caromb, or half an hour to Avignon, which is where tomorrow's itinerary begins.

Santons, Provence's traditional Christmas figures

2. Mt-Ventoux

A visit to Mt-Ventoux, followed by a tour through the glorious gorges of the Nesque valley, plus lunch and shopping for lavender and nougat in the village of Sault.

If your schedule enables you to spend another day in the Vaucluse, try this tour, which takes you to Mt-Ventoux, the *géant* (giant) of Provence, around which many myths and stories have accumulated. The climb from the base of the mountain to the summit at 1,909m (6,233ft) leads you from a Mediterranean to an Alpine landscape, through many transitions of temperature and vegetation.

The first recorded ascent of the mountain was that of the Italian poet Petrarch. He spent part of his childhood in Carpentras and later lived in Avignon. In 1327 he scrambled up the steep slopes in the company of his brother. If you have the time and the energy this is undoubtedly the best way to tackle Mt-Ventoux (detailed information on the routes can be obtained from the local Tourist Office in Bédoin).

The Ventoux is frequently included as one of the stages in the Tour de France cycle race and it was on these steep slopes that the English rider Tom Simpson died in 1967. This ascent is without doubt a *ne plus ultra* for a cyclist, since the steep slope is unremitting and singularly unrelieved by bends.

If cycling isn't your cup of tea, and the infamous Provençal heat is getting you down, do not despair, for the summit can also be reached by car. From Bédoin, you need to take the D974 (direction Chalet Reynard, the base of one of the Ventoux's popular winter ski-stations). The mountain's summit is a further 6km (4 miles) from here.

Though this area, which is known as *l'aire royale du vent et du ciel* (the royal place of wind and sky), is basically rather a mess, you should hardly notice this, since the view is second to none. During the summer the landscape below can be lost in a heat haze and a good case can be made for going up the mountain when the mistral is blowing the skies clear. Of course these

Mt-Ventoux features in the Tour de France

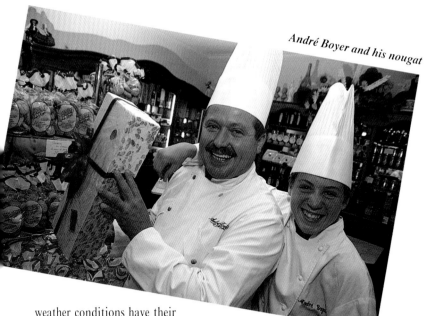

André Boyer and his nougat

weather conditions have their
own perils, notably a considerably lower temperature than down below, and a wind that threatens to toss you
back to Bédoin from whence you came.

Descending from the summit you can reach Bédoin in a circuit
via Malaucène. However, it is much better (even though it might take
you more time) to return the way you came to Chalet Reynard.
Take the D164 (direction **Sault**) and from there descend through
the beautiful but little-known
gorges of the Nesque.

Typically Provençal

These deep valleys number
among Provence's most outstand-
ing natural features. If your schedule allows, stop for a while in
Sault to visit the shop of André
Boyer Maître Nougatier. His delicious nougat is made from a com-
bination of local almonds and
aromatic lavender honey, a speciality of the region.

The **Bar de la Promenade**,
which is located at the south end
of the village *promenade* overlooking the plains is the place in
Sault for a drink and a good cheap
lunch. During late June and early
July the plains are covered in
beautiful purple lavender, which
makes for a delightful view.

3. Papal City and Vineyard Country

This full day's tour begins and ends in Avignon; the morning includes a visit to the Palais des Papes (Popes' Palace), the Doms garden and a walk along the ramparts. Leaving around noon, head for Châteauneuf-du-Pape for a good lunch and numerous wine tastings. From there go to the Pont du Gard, take a kayak down the River Gard and then return to Avignon for a promenade and supper. 80km (50 miles).

If you are coming to Avignon by car, plan to arrive early (by 9am in the summer) and park in one of the free parking areas outside the city walls. The most convenient are the areas by the Porte du Rhône (for visiting the palaces) or at the other end of the city, the Porte de la République, opposite the station. If there is no room in these areas, you can also park inside the walls, though here you will have to pay. The area within the walls is small and easily explored on foot, so taking a car inside is unecessary and best avoided. For the out-of-town (afternoon) part of this itinerary, pack swimwear.

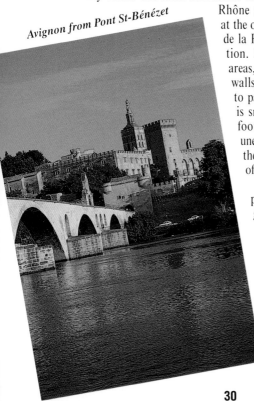

Avignon from Pont St-Bénézet

The town of Avignon occupies a rocky site at the strategic confluence of the Rhône and Durance rivers. The Romans marched past it on the Agrippan Way, following the Rhône valley from Arles to Lyon; later, travellers coming south would take a boat from Lyon to Avignon. The most celebrated arrival was that of Pope John XXII who

Entertainment in Place de l'Horloge

installed himself in Avignon in 1316, placing the town in the full stream of European culture. Although the last pope left Avignon in 1377, the papal legacy is ever present in the city's palaces and vibrant cultural life.

There is an old Provençal proverb that goes: '*Qui s'éloigne d'Avignon perd la raison*,' meaning 'He who leaves Avignon has lost his reason.' This is rather similar to the British saying, 'He who is tired of London is tired of life', and, like London, Avignon is a city that inspires both love and hatred. Petrarch thought the city 'The thoroughfare of vice, the sewers of the earth.' We may have to allow for a little Italian bias here, but by all accounts Avignon had its dark side then and still does. John Evelyn, the English diarist who wrote an account of his travels through Europe in the 17th century, was much impressed with Avignon: 'The walls of the Citty (being all square huge free stone) are absolutely the most neate and best repaire that in my life I ever saw: it is full of well built Palaces.'

The key to liking Avignon today, especially when coming to the city from the languorous countryside, is to be aware that in the summer it seethes with people and heat, reaching a climax during the famed **Festival**

d'Avignon (usually the last three weeks of July and the first week of August). The streets are animated day and night by street performers, musicians and young people from all over Europe. In my view, it is a time to visit but not to stay, unless you love the theatre. There is usually something happening in Avignon, though later in the year the mistral howls through the city, driving street life inside.

Avignon has a north–south axis running from the ramparts of the Palais des Papes, through the Place de l'Horloge, to the Porte de la République at the southern end. The **Place de l'Horloge** is the heart of the city; centre of café life and a popular breakfast spot, it is our first rendez-vous. From the Porte de la République it is a 10-minute walk along the Cours J Jaures and Rue de la République. Stop at the **Tourist Office** to pick up maps and guides.

The main site in Avignon is the monumental **Palais des Papes** (open daily; guided tours and visits with audio guide in several languages; admission fee; tel: 04 90 27 50 74). I can add nothing to the already copious literature on the architecture and history of the palace but I should warn you that you will walk through a succession of empty rooms; only the magnificent friezes and frescos bear witness to the former decorative splendour. It requires a leap of imagination to picture the sumptuous luxury that surrounded the popes. Perhaps the sheer scale of everything is the giveaway; the shopping list for the coronation banquet of Pope Clement VI included: 118 cattle, 1,023 sheep, 101 calves, 914 young goats, 60 pigs, 69 quintals of bacon (a quintal=100kg or 2,200lbs), 1,500 capons, 3,043 hens, 7,428 chickens, 1,195 geese, 50,000 tarts, 6 quintals of almonds, 2 quintals of sugar, 39,980 eggs and 95,000 loaves of 28g (9oz bread). The kitchens are suitably large. Adjacent is the magnificent art collection of the **Petit Palais**, a wealth of medieval paintings and sculptures (open June–Sept closed Tuesday; October–May closed Monday and Tuesday; admission fee; tel: 04 90 86 44 58).

Vines and remains at Châteauneuf

Leaving the palace walk away from the Place de l'Horloge past the cathedral and go up into the **Doms garden,** where you can recover your sense of proportion and admire the view of the Rhône and the **Pont St-Bénézet** – made famous by the song *Sur le Pont d'Avignon.* The bridge is a favourite spot for watching the sun go down (open daily; admission fee; tel: 04 90 27 50 83).

Avignon has a number of good museums, but one that should not be missed is the restored **Musée Calvet** (65 rue Joseph Vernet; closed Tuesday; admission fee; tel: 04 90 86 33 84) a lovely colonnaded building full of tapestries, sculptures, and French paintings of the 18th, 19th and 20th centuries. You can see the only painting by Van Gogh in Provence, *Les Wagons du chemin de fer*, at the **Fondation Angladon-Dubrujeaud** (5 rue Laboureur; closed Tuesday; admission fee; tel: 04 90 82 29 03).

West of Place de l'Horloge are the more expensive shops (furniture, clothing, jewellery), with markets and larger stores to the east. For the moment, however, postpone ideas of shopping, locate the car and set off on the road to **Châteauneuf-du-Pape**.

Once on the ring road, follow signs for Orange and Carpentras. At the first major junction take the left filter onto the N7 (direction Sorgues and Orange). The road crosses the River Ouvèze and shortly afterwards you will see the D17, the first turning for Châteauneuf. I prefer to ignore the D17 and go on to the D192, for this road winds through a small plain of vineyards to the east, slowly revealing Châteauneuf in the distance. The D192 comes to a crossroads where you are faced with a no-entry sign; in fact, you can use this road to gain access to the car park on the right. From here it is a short walk up the hill to the **Place de la Fontaine**, the centre of the village.

The history of Châteauneuf is indissolubly linked with that of Avignon and the 14th-century popes. The château looming over the village, greatly damaged during World War II, was built by the popes as a retreat and summer residence.

The popes are also credited with stirring wider interest in the wines of Châteauneuf. In his story *La Mule du Pape* in *Lettres de Mon Moulin*, Alphonse Daudet wrote of the Avignon pope who every Sunday after vespers rode 12km (7.5 miles) out to the plain around Châteauneuf to survey the progress of the vines he had planted himself and would pass the afternoon in the sun drinking a bottle of local wine – 'that excellent wine, the colour of rubies, which from then on would be called the Châteauneuf-du-Pape'. There are at least 50 major producers of this wine variety and most of them have a *cave* in the village.

Mule-du-Pape *(see page 74)*, a restaurant on the corner of the Place de la Fontaine is a Châteauneuf institution. In the *Restaurant Gastronomique* upstairs, serious food with a Provençal accent is provided, while family cooking (for example an *aïoli* or a *soupe au pistou*) is the order of the day on the terrace downstairs.

After lunch there are a number of options: a walk up to the château, a *dégustation* (wine tasting) or a visit to the interesting wine museum on the premises of the firm Père Anselme. If this is not to your taste then there is an excellent swimming pool near the car park.

Not much later than 3pm you should turn your thoughts to the magnificent **Pont du Gard**. The journey is about 35km (20 miles), leaving on the D17 (direction Orange), and then turning left onto the D976 (direction Roquemaure). Continue in the direction of Remoulins, from where the Pont du Gard is signposted. You are now in the *département* of the Gard, which lies outside the present-day boundaries of the politico-economic region of Provence. However, for the purposes of this guide, it can be argued that the Pont du Gard, as a great Roman construction, is within the context of a larger notion of Provence; certainly it would be a shame to miss it.

The Pont du Gard is an aqueduct spanning the Gard valley. It is the only substantial remains of a system built to carry water the 50km (30 miles) to Nîmes from a spring near Uzès; it has been calculated that its daily flow was somewhere around 200 million litres

(44 million gallons). To me this is an extraordinary tribute to the quality of Roman civilisation.

To see the Pont in the conventional mannner, follow the signs to the car park and walk up. A road bridge was added in the 18th century, enabling you to cross the river under the aqueduct. This in itself is impressive. You can also scramble up the hill to the top of the aqueduct, and at one time you could actually walk across, as the channel was covered to keep the water clean but this is no longer possible. Recent renovation work on the Pont du Gard has created a visitors' centre, Le Portal, an auditorium in a former quarry, a pedestrian promenade and restaurants (all open daily; admission fee; tel 04 66 37 50 99).

Alternatively you could view the acqueduct from a kayak. These can be picked up at Collias – ignore signs for the Pont du Gard and continue on the D981 until you reach the D112 (direction Collias); just before Collias turn left down a narrow lane to the river following signs to **Kayak Vert**. The trip downstream takes about 90 minutes, if you don't get distracted by the beaches and swimming spots. Allow half an hour to get back to the car. Kayak Vert have a courtesy bus from a point just below the bridge. There is no finer or more appropriate way to see the Pont du Gard – built by the Romans to satisfy their vast appetite and love for water – than from the water itself, floating round a bend in the river.

The return to Avignon is quickly done, via Remoulins and the N100 to Villeneuve-les-Avignon. If you have any energy left this is the time to do some shopping.

If you have an extra day in Avignon and it happens to be a Saturday or Sunday, you are within easy reach of two of the best markets in Provence. On Saturday the lovely town of **Uzès** is buried under piles of the best fresh produce, olive oils, soaps and fabrics, and hums with activity (leave Avignon as though returning to the Pont du Gard and continue on the D981 to Uzès). Sunday is the day to visit the famous antique and flea market in **L'Ile-sur-la-Sorgue**, a cool watery town to the east of Avignon (along the N100).

Souvenirs of the bridge

4. Roman Morning, Rural Afternoon

A jam-packed morning exploring Arles' Roman, medieval and folkloric legacy followed by lunch at the nearby Bistro du Paradou. The afternoon is spent buying olive oil from Le Moulin de Maître Cornille and driving through the rural Alpilles to the Cathédrale d'Images and St-Remy. Evening spent in Les Baux. 55 km (34 miles).

Arles' Roman arena

The history of **Arles** and much of its character today was shaped by one major factor: it is situated at the head of the Rhône delta on the route linking Italy with Spain. When Rome came into possession of Spain after the defeat of the Carthaginians, Arles became a key strategic town, linking east and west with the valley of the Rhône.

Its vast **Arena** *(amphithéâtre)* is the most potent witness to that time. While it is worth a visit, you may find this arrangement of huge blocks of stone leaves you unmoved; but go there the day of the bullfight and it will be a different story. All great stadiums are brought alive by the roar of the crowd. The bullfight is one of the great events in Arles and a reminder of its links with Spain.

The other remarkable feature of Arles is the survival of its folk culture, seen in the costumes worn by the Arlesian women. This may lead people to suppose that Arles is the town most representative of Provence, when, in reality, it is

Arlesian folk costume

something of a town apart, shaped primarily by its links with Spain and the Camargue.

I like to park on the Boulevard des Lices in the centre of Arles. You will find it by following signs to the Tourist Office. However, if you are coming from north of Arles on the N570 it is better to park near the Place La Martine or along the river. From here it is a 10-minute walk to the centre of town. On market days parking is more difficult.

Arles has a good system of *forfaits* (inclusive packages) for visiting the museums and monuments. Though I don't propose you visit all the sites it is convenient to buy the *visite générale*. You can buy the ticket at the Muséon Arlaten in the Rue de la République. One museum not to be missed, and key to understanding the history of Arles, is the **Musée de l'Arles Antique** (Avenue de la Première Division Francaise Libre; open daily; admission fee; tel: 04 90 18 88 88). The museum is in a new building, housing numerous antiquities including statues, capitals, carved friezes, pottery, glass, jewellery, mosaics and a large collection of marble sarcophagi.

The **Muséon Arlaten** (29 Rue de la République; open daily July and August, Sept–June closed Monday; tel: 04 90 93 58 11) is also worth a visit. Founded by the great poet Frédéric Mistral, its theme is that of his life's work, a celebration of the people and the traditional ways of life in the South of France – you will notice that every town in the area has its Rue Frédéric Mistral. As you wander through creaking rooms devoted to furniture, religious legends, *santons*, Provençal customs (for example, the female habit of carrying blessed peach stones to guard against bad luck) costumes, tools and *tableaux* of typical scenes and dramas, you will feel you have stepped back in time, a feeling reinforced by the custodians, Arlesian women

Inside St-Trophime

in traditional dress who sit crocheting in corners.

From the museum walk back to the Place de la République where you will see the church of **St-Trophime**. The tympanum of the Last Judgement in the doorway and the cloisters are masterpieces of medieval architecture. English writer Hilaire Belloc described these cloisters in his book *Hills and the Sea*: 'The cloisters are not only the Middle Ages caught and made eternal, they are also a progression of that great experiment from its youth to its sharp close.'

When you come out again into the sunlight walk around the corner to the **Place du Forum**, where Van Gogh painted *Café de la Nuit*. The Place, with cafés and restaurants and the **Nord-Pinus Hotel** where matadors traditionally reside, at one end, is the focal point of the town's cultural life. The Place has two excellent restaurants; Les Vaccares and the Brasserie de Nord-Pinus *(see page 75)*, but unless you are planning to spend the whole day in Arles you should postpone these pleasures – perhaps make a reservation for the evening – and go instead to the Bistro du Paradou for lunch.

Paradou is a 15-minute drive from Arles. Leave the town on the N570 (direction Avignon) and shortly afterwards turn right onto the D17 for Fontvieille and Paradou. There is not a great deal to Paradou other than this one remarkable restaurant, the ultimate French working man's café, where lunch with wine is provided at a fixed price. This is now 190FF (such is the price of fame), including a bottle of house red wine. At the price I don't believe you can eat a better meal in Provence.

The pleasing village of **Mausanne** 2km (1 mile) from Paradou is famous for the quality of its olive oil made at **Le Moulin de Maître Cornille.** The Moulin is only a short way off the main road but the left turn you need to make, though signed, is easy to miss. The mill is a first-class place to buy gifts; in addition to olive oil you can buy soaps made with olive oil, *tapenade* (a creamy paste made

Les Alpilles and the Camargue

12 miles / 7.5 km

from black olives) and jams. The excellent quality of the oil is said to be due to the age of the olive trees – up to 2,000 years (though many were destroyed in the freezing winter of 1956) – and the exceptional dry heat of this area, known as La Vallée des Baux.

Les Alpilles, a chain of hills 25km (15 miles) long and 6–8km (4–5 miles) wide, rise above this valley, a curious misfit in this otherwise flat area and therefore an ideal site for a stronghold such as Les Baux *(see also page 40)*. From the shady streets of Mausanne it is difficult to imagine the existence of this rocky bastion sweltering in the sun only a few kilometres away.

Architectural detail

I would advise against venturing into Les Baux on a hot summer afternoon. You will see the crowds as you approach from Mausanne on the D27. Better to pass a cool half an hour in the **Cathédrale d'Images**, then perhaps go down to St-Remy, returning once more to Les Baux in the early evening.

So, by-passing the village for the time being, continue to the **Cathédrale d'Images** (Val d'Enfer, 13520 Les Baux de Provence; open daily: March–January, 10am–6pm; admission fee; tel: 04 90 54 38 65), on the D27, one bend above Les Baux. In the giant caverns of white stone left by the extraction of bauxite, a rock containing aluminium, images are beamed onto the walls and ceilings by 40 slide projectors, accompanied by music. The project has been brilliantly realised and the effects are stunning. The theme changes every year.

If by now it is late in the day and you are returning to Arles for the evening, you might want to go straight to Les Baux. Otherwise **St-Rémy-de-Provence** is a pleasant 15-minute drive from here

The olive groves are up to 2,000 years old

Santon-making is a local craft

(continue on the D27 and at the bottom of the hill turn right onto the D31). It isn't difficult to pass a couple of hours sitting in the bars on the main boulevard or wandering the streets, trying to resist the gorgeous fabrics in Souleiado's window.

From here there are two alternatives for returning to Les Baux; either take the D5 past the Roman site of Glanum or, more interestingly, return the way you came taking the D31 and D27. You will pass on the left-hand side the workshop where Monsieur Bourges models his *santons*, and as you come over the brow of the hill you have before you the great vista of the Valley of Les Baux with Arles in the far distance.

In the near distance is **Les Baux.** The settlement occupies a prominent place in the mythology of the poetic songsters, the troubadours, and courtly love, which flowered in the courts of the Counts of Provence in the 12th century. The ideal of court life was to live in accordance with a poetic conception of love, which exalted unsatisfied desire – that of the troubador, and by extension that of the knight, for the Lady of the Court. A rather frustrating, if romantic, concept.

The ruins of the castle built by the Lords of Les Baux, where this concept was enacted, occupy the highest point of the site. You will not be disappointed if you make the effort to climb to the highest point of these ruins. Below is the village of Les Baux, a mixture of restored Renaissance houses and ruins. Abandoned in the 17th century, this is now one of the most-visited ancient sites in France. The entrance is via the Musée d'Histoire des Baux/Citadel (Rue de Trencart; open daily; admission fee; tel: 04 90 54 55 56).

To return to Arles, follow the signs to Fontvieille (D17) and turn left when you reach the junction with the N570. An evening in Arles is best spent at one of the restaurants in the Place du Forum, but if you are lucky there may be an event at the **Arena** or at the **Théâtre Antique**.

Les Baux's castle blends into the cliffs

The best way of seeing the Camargue

5. The Camargue

If you leave Arles on the D570 going south, you quickly enter a landscape of lagoons, rice fields and salt marshes, populated by cowboys, bulls and flamingos. This area, contained within the two arms of the Rhône river, is called the Camargue.

The Camargue is an entity the French would call *trés spéciale*. Though part of the *département* of the Bouches-du-Rhône and belonging to the *commune* (district) of Arles, it is a place apart, probably having more rapport with France to the west than the east.

There are really two separate Camargues. One is covered with rice fields, salt pans, stud farms and cattle ranches, and cannot easily be visited. The other is the nature reserve of the **Etang de Vaccarès**. Though containing an extraordinary diversity of wildlife, it is known above all for the flamingos (estimated at 50,000) who rest here in the spring and summer.

The main town of the Camargue is **Les-Saintes-Maries-de-la-Mer**, enshrined in Provençal legend as the landing point of the Boat of Bethany which brought Mary Jacobé (the sister of the Virgin), Mary Salomé, Mary Magdalene and, as one history of Provence has aptly put it, 'half the cast of the New Testament'.

Saintes-Maries-de-la-Mer is an enjoyable town to visit, above all because of the vast beaches – in the summer you should allow at least an hour to travel the 38km (23.5 miles) from Arles. Access to the nature reserve is from the D36.

You should also be aware that the Camargue has no tourist infrastructure, because living here is basically insupportable. The only people who tolerate the conditions are the cowboys, who rear the bulls, and environmentalists. The main plague is the mosquitoes. As a protected environment the Camargue has never been de-mosquitoed. The mosquitoes prey mercilessly on visitors, so take cream with you. The best advice I can give is to go into the Camargue when the mistral is scattering the insects. I think you will find the problems this wind creates with car doors more supportable than the bites.

Aix-en-Provence

6. From the Renaissance to Cézanne

A morning tour of the elegant Renaissance town of Aix and an afternoon exploring Cézanne country.

The first Roman settlement in Provence was founded by the proconsul Sextius Calvinus after his victory over the Franks. He baptised it Aquae Sextiae, a name alluding equally to its founder and the thermal springs near the settlement. It became one of the most important Roman towns in Provence and a major halt on the Aurelian Way, the road connecting the Italian border with the valley of the

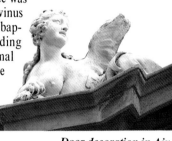

Door decoration in Aix

Rhône. This is the site of **Aix-en-Provence** today. Virtually nothing survives in modern-day Aix from this period of its history. However, the position of Aix on one of the main routes connecting Paris with Nice is a reminder that the main roads of Provence follow the paths of their Roman counterparts.

From the 12th century, when the Counts of Provence had their court at Aix, it developed as a centre of learning and the arts. The university was founded in 1409 by Louis II of Anjou. His second son René, who became Duke of Anjou, Count of Provence (known in Provençal folklore as Good King René), was an enlightened patron of the arts. He made Aix the focal point for artists in Provence, as Avignon had been a century earlier under the popes.

The university and patronage of the arts do more than anything to shape the life of Aix today. The town is full of students and the annual festival of music is said to rival those of Bayreuth and Salzburg (doubtful).

It is relatively easy to find your way in and out

Breakfast at Deux Garçons

of Aix by car. When you reach the ring road follow the signs for the *Office du Tourisme* at Place du Général de Gaulle. The main car parks are located here, close to the fountain marking the western end of the **Cours Mirabeau**, named in honour of the famous Count of Mirabeau of 1789 who was the representative of Aix in Paris. This shaded avenue, with its four fountains and elegant buildings, every other one either a café or a

One of the fountains of Aix

bookshop, is the heart of Aix today. It is a potent symbol of the sophisticated and cultured lifestyle of its inhabitants.

Days in Aix should always begin here, preferably drinking coffee in **Le Café des Deux Garçons** (53*bis* Cours Mirabeau). Long-time meeting-place of writers and intellectuals, its interior is classic 19th-century *brasserie* style, with wooden chairs, marble-topped tables, gilt mirrors and brass lamps.

The Cours Mirabeau was built in the second half of the 17th century as a *cours à carosses,* a street for horse-drawn carriages, a symbol of the increasing prosperity of Aix, capital town of Provence and seat of the court of justice. The area to the south of the Cours, known as the **Quartier Mazarin**, was developed during the 18th century, on the model of an Italian Renaissance town. Fronted by the grand mansions on the Cours – *les hôtels particuliers* – the area rapidly became a fashionable address for the wealthy, who had previously lived in the old town.

One of the finest of the grand mansions in this area is at no 38, Hôtel Maurel de Pontèves. Its façade superimposes the three classical decorative orders – Doric, Ionic and Corinthian – and is notable for the

The decorative Hôtel de Vil[

sculptured figures supporting the balcony above the doorway. The figures represent Atlantis, who in Greek mythology bore the weight of the world on his shoulders. As you walk around the town you will probably notice this classical motif duplicated on numerous smaller balconies.

In the middle of the Cours is a moss-encrusted fountain. Fed by a thermal spring it was originally called the Fontaine Chaude (hot), but is now more often referred to as the mossy fountain, Fontaine Moussue. From here walk down the Rue du 4 Septembre into the Quartier Mazarin. You quickly reach **La Place des Quatre Dauphins**, ornamented by a superb baroque fountain. This is the finest of all the ornamental fountains which adorn Aix.

Walking west from the Place along the Rue Cardinale you come to the **Museé Granet** (Place St-Jean-de-Malte; closed Tuesday; admission fee; tel: 04 42 38 14 70), the most interesting museum in Aix (currently undergoing renovation). The museum houses a fine collection of paintings, including a dozen or so by Cézanne, illustrating the main themes of his work.

Located at the top of Rue Cardinale is Rue d'Italie, where you

A long tradition of sweet-making

will find the Confiserie Brémond Fils, one of the oldest firms making the famous *calissons* of Aix: a boat-shaped confectionery of sweet almond paste blended with crystallised oranges and melons softened in fruit syrup (often apricot). In popular folklore these sweets have attained the status of a kind of Host and are dispensed in church at Christmas, Easter and on 1 September, to commemorate the end of the great plague of 1630.

Crossing Place Forbin, you leave the Mazarin Quarter and enter the old town. This maze of streets north of the Cours Mirabeau is a shoppers' paradise. In the morning the market on the Place Richelme is a colourful sight. Later in the day this is the place to come for bars and it is a relaxed alternative to the Cours. Behind the Post Office – an elegant 18th-century building that once housed the corn market – is **L'Hôtel de Ville**. Built in the 17th century it shows all the decorative motifs of the baroque style: pediments, friezes and the curling forms of flowers and fruit. Inside, the courtyard has a lovely harmony of forms and superb examples of that particularly French urban craft, *ferronnerie d'art* (art metalwork). To the north is **Cathédrale St-Sauveur** with its cloister and Nicolas Froment's 15th-century triptych *Mary in the Burning Bush.* Next door, the Baroque **Palais de l'Archevêché** contains a **Musée des Tapisseries** (Tapestry Museum; closed Tuesday; admission fee; tel: 04 42 23 09 91) and hosts productions in the courtyard during the Festival d'Art Lyrique.

Towards midday in summer the temperature in Aix can climb high and the light becomes very clear – a phenomenon described by Charles Dickens: 'The town was... so hot, and so intensely light, that when I walked out at noon it was like coming suddenly from the darkened room into crisp blue fire. The air was so very clear, that distant hills and rocky points appeared within an hour's walk...'

It may be that Dickens was referring to the distant outline of the **Mont St-Victoire**. It is less than an hour's walk from the centre

Cézanne Country

12 miles / 7.5 km

Itinerary 6
Itinerary 7

Venelles
Vauvenargues
MONT STE. VICTOIRE
Le Tholonet
Puyloubier
Aix-en-
-Provence
St-Antonin-
sur-Bayon
Pourrières
La Barque
Calas
Bouc-
Lel-Air
Fuveau
Cabriès
Gardanne
Peynier
Trets
Les-Pennes-
Mirabeau
Simiane
Collonge
Greasque
Pilon du Roi
▲ 670
Septèmes-
les-Vallons
Peypin
La Bouilladisse
Notre-Dame
Auriol
St-Zacharie
Plan-de-
Cuques
Roquevaire
Marseille
Allauch
Aubagne
Gémenos
Cuges-
les-Pins
La Penne-
s.-Huveaune
Montredon
Carnoux-
en-Provence
Redon
Les Goudes
Cassis
Ceyreste
St-Cyr-
-s.-Mer.
Mediterranean Sea
La Ciotat

of Aix to the foothills of this mountain (15 minutes by car).

Take the ring road as far as the turning for **Le Tholonet**, the D17, known as '*route Cézanne*'. Within minutes the boundaries of Aix are left behind and each bend in the road offers a glimpse of the mountain. When you reach Le Tholonet, you will see on your left a château (the headquarters of La Société du Canal de Provence). On your right is a towering avenue of plane trees leading to a park.

Cézanne never tired of painting this area dominated by the Mont St-Victoire. He wrote to his son: 'I spend every day in this landscape with its beautiful shapes. Indeed I cannot imagine a more pleasant way or place to pass my time.' Le Tholonet presents a number of different options for passing the afternoon. Either you can adjourn to the park, a favourite promenade for the Auxois, or you can take one of a number of walks from various car parks along the D17 between Le Tholonet and Puyloubier. The landscape is fierce and hot in summer, recognisably the one Cézanne shaped on his canvases. Alternatively, you can make a complete circuit (74km/46 miles) of the mountain, via Puyloubier, Pourrières, the D23 (direction Rians), branching left onto the D223 (D10; direction Vauvenargues) and from there back to Aix along the D10. The journey will take you through spectacular rocky landscapes, the vineyards of the Côte de Provence estates and give you a view of the north face of the mountain. This area so captivated Pablo Picasso that he bought the château

Picasso's château at Vauvenargues

in Vauvenargues (unfortunately this site is not open to the public). For a complete circuit bringing you back to the Cours Mirabeau you should allow around two hours.

You should be back in Aix in time for an apéritif and the *promenade* on the Cours, and perhaps supper at the **2G** (the familiar name for the Café des Deux Garçons), where you breakfasted.

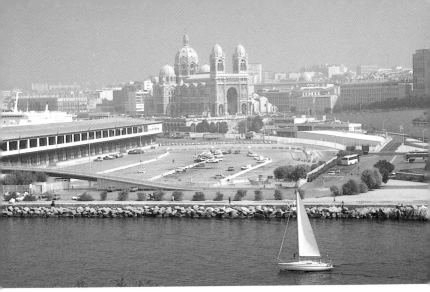

France's second city, Marseille

7. Marseille

Marseille, France's second city after Paris, is less than 30 minutes' drive from Aix-en-Provence (by way of the A51 motorway). It can be seedy, as every port city, though it is currently undergoing something of a renaissance. The contrasts with the sedate splendour of Aix are marked, though the inhabitants of Marseille are supremely laid-back.

The appeal of Marseille is unconventional. If you are going to pay a short evening or morning visit, here are a few reference points. The restaurants of the Vieux Port are famous for the Marseille dish *bouillabaisse*; Miramar, in particular, is an institution *(see page 76)*. Place Thiars, just off the southeast corner of the port, has restaurants and clubs open all night. The other main location for restaurants and bars, trendier than the port, is the **Cours Julien**, a 15-minute walk from the old port up La Canebière (the latter is the most famous street in the city and a symbol of Marseille, in the way, for example, that Fifth Avenue is a symbol of New York.)

The best strategy for a short visit is to explore the area of the Vieux Port, then go out to the Palais du Pharo, on the spur of the port, for a great view over the city. From here drive along the Corniche President J. F. Kennedy to the Vallon des Auffes, an old Mediterranean fishing port, where you will find several good fish restaurants.

On the quay

ALONG THE COAST

In 1887 the French writer Stephen Liégeard, inspired by the deep blue of the southern French coast, came up with the enduring headline, *La Côte d'Azur* (Azure Coast). Though this describes the whole coastal area equally well, the coast within the compass of this guide – from Marseille to St-Tropez – is more generally known as *La Côte Provençale*. If you want to go further east along the coast to Cannes and Nice, I recommend you buy a copy of either *Insight Guide: French Riviera* or the *Insight Pocket Guide: French Riviera*.

The three itineraries that follow have selected highlights from the Côte Provençale and each could easily make a day. The overall scheme is linear, linking Cassis and St-Tropez, two towns connected by 100km (60 miles) of twisting coastal roads; a magnificent drive on a crisp winter's day, a crawling caravan of traffic in summer.

By the end of the year 2000 it was calculated that of the 25 million visitors to Provence, two-thirds came to the coast and the majority of those in the summer months. A quick, impressionistic tour of the coast can, of course, be made in the high season, but I fear the impression would not be a good one. My advice, if you only have one day in the summer, is to enjoy one good itinerary. And always have a swimming costume at the ready.

Boats of all sizes along the Côte Provençale

8. Cassis

This itinerary consists of a trip to the busy old port of Cassis, messing about in boats in the beautiful 'calanques', a fish lunch in one of numerous great-value restaurants down by the port and some shopping for fine wines.

Cassis is 30 minutes by motorway from Aix-en-Provence; leave Aix on the A8 (direction Fréjus/Nice), turn south onto the A52 (direction Aubagne and then Toulon), take the last exit for Cassis, entering the town on the D559. Parking is never easy but early in the morning you should find a space in the car park next to the port.

The three things I believe should shape any visit to Cassis are: a swim in the wonderful waters of the fjord-like *calanques (see next page)*, a fish lunch in the port and a taste of the aromatic white wines produced in the surrounding hillsides.

The port of Cassis has a feeling of expectancy in the morning. Fishermen are landing the catch from the previous night under the careful eye of the restaurant proprietors and the boats that ply up and down the local coast are waiting to begin their daily shuttles. You can pick up a list of the trips on offer from a hut on the quay and then plan your morning over a coffee in one of the port's many bars.

Between Cassis and Marseille the coastline is a massive series

Fish on the move in Cassis

'Calanque' boat trip

of limestone cliffs, rising as high as 400m (1,300ft), indented with long, narrow channels of water – known as *calanques*. They were formed when the sea invaded the narrow river valleys between these cliffs at the end of the Ice Age. Some of them end in a small beach, others are hemmed in by white walls of rock that rise sheer from the water. The water has both a translucence and a density of colour that is astonishing. The cost of visiting the *calanques* depends both on which ones you choose and for how long you go. The nearest ones to Cassis are Port-Miou, Port Pin and d'en Vau. Make sure that you take a boat that stops for swimming.

The *calanques* can also be visited on foot. The Tourist Office will give you a map of the *randonnée* (hikes) in the area, though you will probably find the paths are closed during the summer due to the ever-present fire risk.

Aim to return from the *calanques* in time for a fish lunch in the port. The **Quai des Baux** has a great line of venues, notably L'Oustau de la Mer, Bar le Port, César and Chez Gilbert.

If you are staying in Cassis and would like an afternoon excursion or you are moving down the coast in the direction of Bandol, you should take *la route des Crêtes*, the D141 to La Ciotat, along the magnificent cliffs of **Cap Canaille**. This

'La route des Crêtes' to Bando

road also has the advantage of passing the **Clos Ste-Magdeleine**, where one of the finest white wines of Cassis is produced. The road twists for 13km (8 miles) up to the **Sémaphore du Bec de l'Aigle** – Eagle's Beak Point – where a vertiginous view offers you the whole of this unique coastline.

From Eagle's Beak Point follow the D40 until it links up with the D559 to Bandol. The town of **Bandol**, a seemingly endless seafront of bright boutiques and crowded beaches, you can safely bypass; the wines of Bandol you cannot. The town gives its name to one of the really great red wines of Provence and to one of the finest rosé wines in the world. The rosé somehow manages to be both light and full-bodied, the best of all drinks on a hot summer day. It can be hard to find as the best producers jealously guard their Mourvèdre grapes for the rich red wines with their complex bouquets of fruit and herbs.

Many of the producers are located near the medieval villages of **La Cadière d'Azur** and **Le Castellet**; you will see signs for them before Bandol. They are more marked by the demands of tourism than the perched villages in the Vaucluse, but camped high in the hills they have the usual commanding views.

My favourite Bandol producer is **Domaine Tempier** (just off the D82 north of the city map), where you are guaranteed a warm welcome from the Peyraud family and a good *dégustation*.

9. Ile de Porquerolles

The Ile de Porquerolles is the largest of the three **Iles d'Hyères**. These islands are an image of an older Mediterranean coast – a coast that was sparsely populated and densely forested, with beaches that are just a dash of sand separating trees and water. The easiest and cheapest way to reach Porquerolles is by ferry from the **Presqu'ile de Giens**, near Hyères. If you are coming from the direction of Bandol there is no need to go into Hyères. After the port of Toulon, take the D559 to Carqueiranne and cross to the Presqu'ile on the isthmus behind the Plage de l'Almanarre. Windsurfers note: this beach has the best conditions in the south of France.

The ferries leave from **La Tour Fondue** every day of the year to serve the island's permanent population of 300 people. In July and August they run every thirty minutes between 8.30am and 8pm; at other times check the timetables (tel: 04 94 58 21 81). The service takes approximately 20 minutes and the round trip costs 87FF. (It's only worth paying the charge for bicycles if you have a mountain bike, as the paths are too rough for tourers.)

A sailboarder's mecca

The island is 7km (4 miles) long and 3km (2 miles) wide, well within the scope of walkers. The ideal mode of transport is the mountain bike. They can be hired from the village of Porquerolles (about 75FF a day), though demand exceeds supply in the summer. Before I leave you to enjoy this lovely island here are a few tips: pick up a map of the island from the Tourist Office and collect provisions before leaving the village; there is no water on the island and no beach cafés once you leave the vicinity of the port.

Finally, ensure you have enough time to get back for the last ferry.

10. St-Tropez

St-Tropez – the Vieux Port, the village, the Citadel; Pampelonne and its famous beaches; the hill towns of Gassin and Ramatuelle; the wines of Château Minuty; the Place des Lices and the Café des Arts.

A brief history: from time immemorial St-Tropez has been a village of the sea, home of fishermen, mariners and privateers. The port is an excellent mooring. In 1892 Paul Signac, the pontillist painter, came to St-Tropez and stayed, bewitched by the light, the deserted beaches and the little village of fishermen. The writer Colette lived here in the 1920s, already complaining of the crowds. During World War II, on 15 August 1944, the port was mined and destroyed; 3,000 parachutists landed in the town, while the Americans landed on the beach of Pampelonne.

The 1960s heralded Brigitte Bardot and the filming of *And God Created Woman*. St-Tropez became known internationally and its demise was forecast regularly during the 1960s, 70s and 80s. But today it is enduringly popular. Why? I think because it manages to be both a Provençal fishing village and port, and the very image of the *dolce vita*. The Place des Lices is the rendezvous for the local *boulistes* and where the celebrities come for an *apéritif*. The Baie de Pampelonne is filled with expensive boats and beautiful people; the sandy beach 5km (3 miles) long, is backed not by a concrete jungle but by farms and vineyards. Then there is the port and the nightlife. In this setting everyone has a chance to live out their

Beach bar, St-Tropez

dreams. I consider St-Tropez one of the great places of France, but in summer it needs to be approached with care.

If you are just coming here for one day, try to arrive before 9am and leave after 10pm – a good day in St-Tropez is a long one. The N98 into St-Tropez divides into a one-way system as you reach the town; follow this until you reach Place Blanqui where you will see signs for the large Parking du Port. It is rarely a good idea to take your car further than this. You can get a good map from the Tourist Office on the Quai Jean Jaurès in the old port.

The morning is the time to wander past the boats that embellish the *quai* and to drink a *café glacé* in one of the famous bars, such

View from the Citadel

as **Sénéquier** or **Le Gorille**. Never seeming to move, these boats are an essential part of the show. From the *quai* walk into the heart of the old village via Place de la Mairie. The village is a nocturnal creature in summer and you will find the shops gingerly opening their doors only at 10am.

Around 11 o'clock you should be thinking of leaving for the beaches, but first it is worth walking up to the **Citadel**, the old fort above St-Tropez. As you look over the tiled roofs and the clock tower to the Gulf of St-Tropez, it is easy to understand why the town has become such an icon of the South of France. Try and visit the Musée de l'Annonciade near the old port, with its excellent collection of modern masters, many of whom painted in St-Tropez (closed Tuesday; admission fee; tel: 04 94 97 04 01).

St-Tropez has two beaches within walking distance, the Plage des Graniers and the Plage des Canebiers, but for *le total* (total nudity), you must drive round to the **Plage de Pampelonne** (from the car park head out of the town and after about 1km (⅝ mile)

Tahiti-Plage

turn right onto the D93 *route des Plages*). As you drive along the *route des Plages* you will see signs for **Tahiti-Plage, Bora-Bora, Club 55, Nioulargo,** some of the famous concessions occupying the majority of the beach. A hedonistic day at one of these with a sun-lounger, parasol, the service of the *plagiste*, lunch and car parking will probably not cost less than 500FF per person. You can of course put your towel down on the public beaches and pick a concession for lunch. As a general rule the beaches are less crowded the further you move away from St-Tropez.

If by 5pm you find the charms of the beach are palling, or the heat is overbearing, the late afternoon sea breezes will be cooling **Ramatuelle** and **Gassin**, two hill towns situated behind Pampelonne. Gassin, perhaps the finer of the two, though less of a living village than Ramatuelle, has the advantage of being home to **Château Minuty** (on the D61 between Gassin and St-Tropez), a beautiful estate producing some of the finest wines in the Côte de Provence. The white and rosé wines designated *cuveé de l'Oratoire* are extremely special.

If at all possible, I'd recommend avoiding St-Tropez between the hours of 5pm and 8pm, when it is far more pleasant to be walking in the vineyards of Château Minuty. For me this is the low point of St-Tropez's day – hot and crowded. One fine option is to have an early supper in the cool perfection of Gassin. However, you must be back in time to witness an important part of the St-Tropez experience: the evening promenade in the **Place des Lices** with an apéritif or a coffee in the **Café des Arts**.

Place des Lices by night

11. A Circuit in the Hills

A day's ride through forests of pine and oak, vineyards and olive trees; stopping to see the Château of Entrecasteux; swim in a waterfall and visit the market town of Aups. 60km (37 miles).

This part of the Var, whilst recognisably a part of the Provence you have been travelling through, is in many ways different. The first thing you will notice as you cross the A8 *autoroute du soleil* (the great divide in Provence) is the change in the pace of life; it is slow. This is a rural area but it is without the great agricultural riches of the alluvial plains which surround the Rhône. The forests of pine and oak are broken by vineyards and olive trees but not by endless fields of melons. As a result the culinary tradition is poorer, it is the *soupe au pistou* and the *aioli*, and the superb menu for just 100FF becomes increasingly difficult to find.

Similarly the wine is much poorer than closer to the Rhône, each village has a co-operative, but the wines are not of a high quality. Domaine St-Jean and Château Thuerry in Villecroze, producing good, sometimes excellent, red and rosé wines, are the only estates worth a special visit.

The villages are simpler than those in the Bouches-de-Rhône, the masons not having around them the tremendous forms of the Romans, who merely passed by this area as they hurried along the Aurelian Way from Fréjus to Aix. But they have their own charm, their *cours*, cafés and *boulistes* and their superb *campaniles* – the structures of ornamental metalwork that adorn the ubiquitous bell towers and cage the bells.

Climbing up into the Var

Salernes is a good starting point. From the direction of St-Tropez it is a 30-minute drive from Le Muy (at the junction of the

Window in Salernes

D25 and the A8/N7 via the N555 to Draguignan and the D557 then turn left on D560. At first sight there is nothing remarkable about Salernes; it only really gets going when the *cours* is filled by the market on Wednesday and Sunday. However, it is identified in France (and world-wide) with the superb work of its *céramistes*. At one time as many as 50 factories were producing *tomettes*, the small red hexagonal tiles that cover the floors in nearly all the older houses in Provence. Today the local clays are not only turned into *terre cuit* for floors; the glazes and designs of the ceramicists transform the humble clay into superb decorative objects – tiles for kitchens and bathrooms, lamps and bowls. You will see the showrooms as you approach Salernes on the D560; they are interesting to visit and great for presents.

From Salernes it is 8km (5 miles) to **Entrecasteaux** along the D31, which follows the winding course of the River Bresque. Just out of Salernes you will see on the right-hand side a series of pillars clothed in mauve tiling marking the atelier and showroom of Alain Vagh, one of the 15 ceramic manufacturers in Salernes. His passion is to clothe everything with tiles; his jeep and grand piano have already suffered this fate.

As you turn the corner by the football pitch the massive **Château d'Entrecasteaux** (enquire at the Tourist Office for guided tours of the château) comes into view, bearing down on the small village of the same name. It was originally an 11th-century fortress, but the classically simple facade you see today dates from the 17th and 18th centuries, when it hosted among others the diarist Madame de Sévigné. Perhaps the most interesting part of its history is that you wouldn't see it at all today if it had not been rescued from ruin in 1974 by a Scotsman, Ian McGarvie-Munn. The restored château has a light, modern interior that is minimally furnished. Though interesting, you might think the entrance price excessive to view rooms decorated in non-

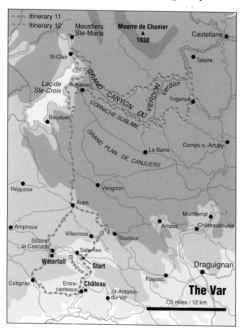

period style. You may prefer to contemplate the vagaries of history and drink a beer in one of the bars opposite the château, before lunching in Cotignac.

The road to Cotignac (D50) comes up as a sharp right turn shortly after you leave Entrecasteaux. It winds for 8km (5 miles) through vineyards that just sneak into the Côtes de Provence appellation. You will see the big wine cooperative as you come into **Cotignac**. Turn left at this point, drive towards the main *cours* and leave the car in the car park on the left. From here you will enter the village at the bottom of its magnificent central *cours*, one of the finest in the Var, shaded by huge plane

trees and surrounded by houses dating from the 16th, 17th and 18th centuries. Before settling down to lunch it is also worth walking up to the Place de la Mairie to take a look at the marvellous *campanile*.

Alain Vagh has tiled his jeep

The small market town of **Aups**, situated at the foot of the mountain of the Espiguières (one of the first spurs of the Alps), is your next destination. The D22 from Cotignac to Aups passes through **Sillans-la-Cascade** where, just under a kilometre (⅝ mile) from the village, the River Bresque falls 45m (150ft) over a cliff into a deep pool. This is a well-known beauty spot and it is usually pretty crowded during the summer months; however, the walk is enjoyable, and the water is cold, making it a good place for a refreshing swim. The path to the waterfall leaves the village from the corner of the road immediately opposite the restaurant Les Pins.

Aups, as befits the chief town of the area, is a bustling place. In summer it is one of the few towns filled with visitors. In the winter it puts on another hat, and devotes itself to *la chasse* (the hunt);

every restaurant has wild boar pâté and rabbit stew on its menu and the streets are empty. You should enjoy walking around Aups; the air is very pure and the light has excellent luminosity. The last time I was in Aups I bought a few bottles of red wine from Maurice Chauvin, whose *cave* is in Avenue Marechal Joffre. Chauvin makes an old style *vin du table*, fruity and natural, producing around 2,000 bottles a year from his small vineyards – he is one of the few remaining farmers who are licensed to sell their wine. For me he typifies Aups: he welcomes visitors in summer but remains true to the traditional ways of life.

When you leave Aups, no matter where you are staying, you should drive the 10km (6 miles) along the D77 to **Tourtour**. The name of the village is said to derive from the Celtic word 'tur', meaning highest point, and if you go up to the highest point by L'Eglise St-Denis (towards sunset is the perfect time or when the mistral is sweeping the skies clear), you will be rewarded with a stunning sight. The village has built a very fine new observation point locating surrounding landmarks. The *place du village*, with the fountain in the middle, is a tempting place to have a drink and a meal. But if the day has not rolled on too quickly the last stop of the day is only a hairpin bend or two away on the D51.

Villecroze-les-Grottes has none of the obvious glories of Tourtour, though the park and the old village are certainly worth visiting: note

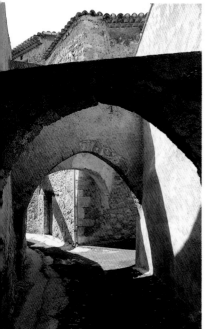

the massive walls of the château and the fountain in the wall in Rue de France. Above all in Villecroze you get the feeling that life being lived to the full. The bars are busy (a chess game is usually in progress, since there is a long tradition of chess-playing in this town), and the *boulistes* are invariably playing in the finely proportioned *cours*, bounded on one side by the village school. If you time your visit right, the music academy will be hosting a concert or the town's famous rugby team will be playing a match in Villecroze. If none of these things are hapening, however, don't despair – the **Bar la Cascade** is a good spot to end the day with a drink and a meal.

Villecroze-les-Grottes

12. A Lake and a Canyon

A 99-km (60-mile), three-hour circuit that leaves from Aups and takes in the Lac de Ste-Croix and the breathtakingly beautiful Grand Canyon du Verdon, one of Provence's most notable natural wonders.

Aups is frequently referred to as the 'gateway to the Alps', because the D957 leaving the town to the north climbs very rapidly into high mountain country. Within the space of around 30 minutes, you should reach the limits of the Var, and if you drive across the Pont du Galetas at the bottom of the Grand Canyon du Verdon you will make your first entrance into the *département* of the Alpes de Haute-Provence.

The Grand Canyon du Verdon is one of the great natural sights in Europe, a savage slash in the earth, measuring 21km (13 miles) long and at times no more than 6m (18ft) wide, compressed between vertiginous rock faces rising as high as 700m (2,296ft).

The instrument of this work is the Verdon River, now regulated by dams at Chaudanne and Castellane and flowing peacefully into the **Lac de Ste-Croix**.

A complete circuit of the canyon will normally take around three hours, depending on how many of the excellent photographic opportunities you manage to resist. It is rumoured that in August the volume of traffic can stretch this to 5 hours. If you are coming from Aups, the best point of attack is probably Aiguines. From here follow the D71, known as the *corniche sublime*. Constructed in 1925 to serve the new obsession with touring by motor car, the *corniche* is designed to render the full effect of the canyon. It succeeds magnificently.

The Grand Canyon du Verdon

From the D71 take the D90 to Trigance and then the D955 until the junction with the D952, the old Castellane road. At St-Clair, 33km (20 miles) later, turn left onto the D957 returning to Aups.

The LUBERON

13. Le Pays d'Apt

Perched villages – Roussillon, Gordes, Bonnieux; Cistercian simplicity and splendour; glacé fruits and the fruity wines of the Côtes de Luberon. Approximately 70km (45 miles).

From a base in Apt the day is a roller-coaster ride through a small area bounded on one side by the Plateau de Vaucluse and on the other by the mountains of the Luberon. This area is generally known as the Luberon, though locally it is referred to as Le Pays d'Apt.

Apt was a considerable Roman colony, situated on the route of the Domitian Way, the great road connecting the Alpine towns of Sisteron and Briançon to the northeast with the Rhône valley. Just 16km (10 miles) west of Apt, where the Domitian Way crossed the River Calavon, you can see the Pont Julien, one of the best-preserved Roman bridges in France. As you travel through this region you will be constantly reminded of past cultures.

The Luberon also has great agricultural riches. Screened from the mistral by the hills of the Vaucluse it has the ideal climate for fruit growing and has made Cavaillon (on the western edge of the Luberon) into France's great fruit market. If you enter the Pays d'Apt from the *arrière pays* (back country) of the Var you will see the transition from endless forest to line after line of fruit trees.

Market in Apt

Mural in Roussillon

The town of Apt is in permanent anticipation of Saturday, when the centre of gravity of the Luberon tilts east and the streets are filled with a maelstrom of marketeers. You will not find much to detain you on other days but it is a good base from which to explore the Luberon, as you can generally find a hotel room without booking months in advance. A coffee in the **Café Gregoire**, opposite the Tourist Office on Place de la Bouquerie, will set you up for the day.

Apt is famous for its glacé fruits in the way that Aix is famous for its *calissons* – both make good presents. You will pass the **Aptunion** factory on your way to Roussillon about 3km (2 miles) outside Apt on the N100. It has a retail outlet selling the many varieties of glacé fruits as well as other classic Provençal products. Shortly after the factory, you will see the first signs for **Roussillon**. The most spectacular approach is from the D227 (the third turning to Roussillon off the D4 from the direction of Apt), the village coming into view on a precipitous cliff that has lent its many hues of red to the *crépi* (cement rendering) of the houses.

The position of Roussillon is probably more spectacular now than when it was built, for two centuries of commercial exploitation of the ochre deposits have left it surrounded by red quarries and cliffs. They can be explored by a footpath that leaves from behind the car park on the east side of the village, though they are best avoided if it is very hot or wet. You should not miss the huge panorama over the Ventoux and the Luberon from the *platform du rocher* at the top of the village. To the northwest you can see the town of **Gordes**, built on a promontory of rock at the foot of the plateau of the Vaucluse.

Gordes is dominated by its castle and church, best seen from the approach road (D15); however, before entering the town you might like to visit **Les Bories**, which you will see signposted from the road.

Bories are dry stone huts built by marginally overhanging each course of stones so that the walls incline towards a point, where large slabs of stone can bridge the gap, ensuring they remain watertight. The *bories* were constructed and lived in by peasants, who needed temporary shelter to be near their flocks and crops. It is estimated that there are as many as 6,000 of them in Provence, the majority of them isolated but occasionally found in groups, such as this one near Gordes. The *bories* are now home to a museum of rural life (daily 9am–sunset).

Les Bories

Archaeological evidence suggests that Neolithic man lived in structures similar to *bories*, which were reconstructed and then copied over the centuries in a simple continuity of tradition – a tradition being continued in a curious way by the people restoring *bories* as second homes.

You can park in the middle of Gordes and, although it is crowded in the summer, this is probably a better bet than a hot walk up the hill. If you have visited the *bories* you will be in need, almost certainly, of a drink or two. The **Café de la Renaissance** in the small *place* behind the castle is likely to be welcome. Here, in the shadow of the walls, you can weigh the pros and cons of visiting the castle. The pros: the entrance is right in front of you, the castle contains a fine Renaissance fireplace and the views from the battlements are superb. The cons: the castle was extensively damaged during World War II, then scrupulously restored from ruin by the Op-art artist Victor Vasarely and now exhibits modern art. If you come out in favour of eating an early lunch in the Renaissance then that might not be a bad choice *(see page 77)*.

Before you leave Gordes in the afternoon it is worth casting an eye over the **church of St-Firmin**. Built in the 18th century it is remarkable for having retained its original polychrome decoration.

In the 12th century France saw the founding of the second great monastic order, the Cistercian, by monks anxious to return to the original strictness of the Benedictine rule. Their leader, St-Bernard, espoused solitude and silence and favoured architecture of simple, harmonious forms to facilitate contemplation. They began to build abbeys which would conform to these ideals and one of them was in the isolated Sénancole valley near Gordes.

The abbey of **Sénanque** (4km/2 miles from Gordes on the D177) in the Sénancole valley is a sight for sore eyes. When you look at it from the east over the lavender fields it has a perfection of form that is unforgettable. Even if you go no further than this point the journey will have been worthwhile.

The monks have recently returned and the abbey can be visited (10am–noon and 2–6pm, except for Sunday am and the mornings of religious feasts). The restored building you see on the right-hand side of the valley is the refectory, housing an exhibition devoted to the life of the Cistercian order.

It is now time to travel to the **perched villages** on the opposite side of the valley: Oppède, Ménerbes, Lacoste, Bonnieux, whose names make up the modern litany of the Luberon. They have – along with the other villages of the Luberon – a turbulent history. Many were partly destroyed in the religious conflicts of the 16th century, but Bonnieux enjoyed great prosperity as a papal fiefdom until the Revolution. By the 1950s they were falling into ruin, ravaged by time and rural depopulation. At this point they were 'rediscovered' by artists and writers looking for an idyllic rural habitat, and the process of restoration began. Today there is hardly a house to be restored, and though visitors course through the narrow streets the villages have certainly not lost their appeal.

All of the above villages can be recommended for one reason or another but I have picked out **Bonnieux**, for the fine views across the valley over to Lacoste, the steep streets bordered by grand *hôtel particuliers*, the **Musée de la Boulangerie** (bakery museum) and an excellent producer of Côtes de Luberon wine.

From Gordes, Bonnieux is around 21km (13 miles) away. To get there, take the D2 (direction Cavaillon), turn left onto the D103 (direction Beaumettes), turn left onto

St-Firmin

the N100 and then turn right to Bonnieux on the D36.

It's not always easy to find parking in Bonnieux, but the nearer you manage to park to the Hôtel César – on the right as you come through the village – the less you will have to climb. Opposite the César a cobbled street runs to the top of the village. Continue up Rue de la République and you will arrive first to Rue de la Marie, leading to the *belvédére* and a lovely view out over the Luberon.

Located further up Rue de la République, at number 12, is the Musée de la Boulangerie (Bakery Museum). The museum has been well put together, although it is disappointing in some details: I would have liked more information on types of bread and the skills of the *boulanger*. As a friend remarked, a museum of the Marquis de Sade – who lived in Lacoste – might have been more interesting.

My great discovery in Bonnieux is the **Château la Canorgue** and its fine wines. The château is located a little way past the wide corner at the bottom of the village, along the D149 (direction Pont Julien). The château is archetypical Provence, fading yellow in a shady courtyard with an overgrown ornamental basin in the garden below. The wines produced are atypical of the region, in that red, white and róse are all good. The delicious white wine has a surprising length of fruit and the reds keep extremely well.

Château la Canorgue

With a few bottles of wine in the boot of your car, you might like to finish the day by staying on the D149 to the **Pont Julien** and then, if the time is right, go back to the D4 and find a point where you can watch the setting sun turn the gorgeous ochre hues of Roussillon to gold.

Shopping

Shopping in Provence is one of the best way of meeting the people who live here. I say meeting them because Provence is not the sort of place where you "grab and buy". Shopping is often a slow process; whether you are a profitable visitor or a regular customer, the social aspect of buying takes precedence over the commercial. In the *boucherie*, for example, the prolonged discussion of the relative merits of this week's *gigot* (lamb), is considered more crucial than serving the long queue, and in *caves* (wine cellars) vintners are always happy to sell a few bottles but they are often keener for you to discuss last year's vintage.

Eye-catching display

Each itinerary in this book notes the characteristic product of a region or town, and suggests a place to buy it; *calissons* (a confection of fruit and almonds) in Aix-en-Provence, wine in Gigondas, ceramics in Salernes, olive oil in Les Alpilles. The excellent shops of Avignon are only briefly mentioned in passing, there being more important items on the menu for that day. A morning among the splendid architecture of the streets and squares of Aix-en-Provence is a shopping trip with an unusual cultural dimension.

Markets

Markets *(see page 69)* are the life-blood of the small producer and the cornerstone of local economies in Provence. They are also social occasions of the first importance, when people come in from the

Market produce

surrounding countyside to review the progress of the *primeurs* and to bemoan the mistral, perhaps drink an *apéritif* or just chat.

Most villages have a weekly market that takes place through the year, on a day that is as fixed as the traffic jam on the *autoroute du soleil* on the first weekend in August. The stall holders will be local producers of fruit and vegetables, chickens and eggs, honey and *chèvre* (goat's cheese); garlic and olive merchants (the latter often having as many as 30 types of olives – *noires aux herbes, farcies aux anchois, cassées pimentées, speciales apéritif ail-piment*); herbalists and the travelling *charcutières* (butchers) and general tradespeople who move within a local sphere of markets.

There are also the great regional markets which stallholders travel considerable distances to reach. These include the Saturday market in the town of Arles and the markets of Isle-sur-la-Sorgue, Apt and Vaison-la-Romaine. In addition to all the agricultural produce for sale you can find Provençal cloths and *la faïence* (local ceramics).

Souleiado to take home

The markets are the clearest indication of the relative wealth and resources of each area. You will notice, for example, how the super-abundant cheapness of fruits and vegetables in the markets of the Bouches-du-Rhône diminishes as you travel into the Var.

Souleiado

The 300-year-old Provençal tradition of hand-printing fabrics is still carried on by one remaining firm,

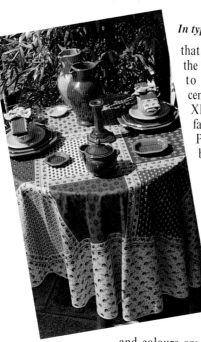

In typical colours

that of Souleiado in Tarascon. Many of the prints are Indian in origin, brought to France at the end of the 17th century to decorate the court of Louis XIV, *le roi soleil*. The colours of the fabrics are derived from the hues of Provence, notably ochres, yellows, blues and greens.

The Souleiado name gained international renown during the 1950s, when Pablo Picasso and the writer/artist Jean Cocteau adopted their shirts. Nowadays, it has the cachet (and prices) of a name such as Hermès. Souleiado has shops in all the main towns and even in some of the smaller, wealthier ones, such as Gordes.

Although the Souleiado designs and colours are indisputably magnificent, similar designs are mass produced and available at much cheaper prices. Larger markets have stalls selling these fabrics by the metre. Souleiado patterns can be seen all over Provence, on upholstery, tableware and as clothes.

Faïence in Provence

The art of shaping and baking clay has been known in Provence since the Middle Ages and has developed in a number of ways. One of the most sophisticated is *faïence*, the polychrome decoration of clay plates and bowls. Since the 17th century the potters of Moustiers-Sainte-Marie have held a reputation for being masters of this craft. You will find their work and that of other *faïenciers* sold across Provence. Other products of this tradition are the tiles and ceramics of Salernes and the *santons* (clay figures), sold in many pottery shops but bought ideally from a small atelier, such as the one on the road from St-Rémy to Les Baux.

Wine

Visiting private estates and farms to taste and purchase wines is not normally categorised as shopping, probably because it is much too pleasurable. However, there are many excellent wines to buy across Provence, particularly in the viticultural region of the southern Rhône. A good bottle of wine is one of the most potent reminders of Provence you can have in your shopping bag.

Market day at Apt

Markets

The following is a list of market days across the region. Trips to smaller towns, in particular, tend be enriched if they coincide with market day in that town.

Every day
Marseille-Noailles (vegetables)
Aix-en-Provence (Place Richelme)
Avignon

Sunday
Avignon-Porte Magnanen
Isle-sur-la-Sorgue
Salernes

Monday
Bédoin
Les-Saintes-Maries-de-la-Mer

Tuesday
Cotignac
Gordes
St-Tropez
Vaison-la-Romaine

Wednesday
Arles
Aups

Roussillon
Sault
St Remy

Thursday
Ramatuelle

Friday
Carpentras
Les-Saintes-Maries-de-la-Mer

Saturday
Avignon-Porte Magnanen
Aix-en-Provence
Apt
Arles
Aups
Bonnieux
St-Tropez
Uzès

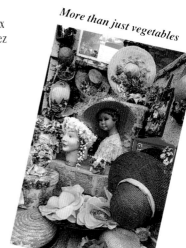

More than just vegetables

Eating Out

What is classic Provençal cuisine? As with all questions of this type regarding definitions of Provence it is hard to answer because the pages of the Provençal cookbook bear the same polyglot imprint as the rest of the culture. It is the cooking of a fairly impoverished region enriched by ingredients from the surrounding Mediterranean cultures: pasta, polenta, *soupe au pistou* (a kind of clear vegetable soup with the Provençal version of pesto added) from Italy; *crudités* and small vegetable appetisers from Spain; and *couscous* and *merguez* (spiced sausages) from North Africa.

The essential elements of Provençal cooking can be summed up as the use of olive oil, the dominance of vegetables, except in winter, when the spoils of the *chasse* – small birds, rabbits and wild boar – dominate the table, and the use of herbs and garlic for seasoning. The latter is far less common than is supposed and I doubt if anyone would now suffer the fate of Smollett: 'I was almost poisoned with garlic, which they mix in all their ragouts, and all their sauces; nay, the smell of it perfumes the very chambers, as well as every person you approach.'

At its best Provençal cooking is a natural and seasonal cuisine, retaining the taste and texture of simple, fresh ingredients from the countryside and the sea. This was probably quite a revelation when Provence was first 'discovered'. Even in the 1950s cooking was generally much heavier, with a greater reliance on sauces, as fresh ingredients were harder to come by. As a result, the

Provençal fare

simple country cooking of a poor region was accorded an almost mythical status and exaggerated claims were made in its favour.

A good example of this is the *aïoli*. *Aïoli* is a garlic mayonnaise that usually accompanies a plate of cooked vegetables, always potato, carrots and beans, served with a piece of cod and perhaps some snails and a hard-boiled egg. Now this was clearly designed as a poor man's dish. The cod was used because it retains its freshness longer

than other fish, but by the time it reached the back country of Provence the pungent garlic sauce was probably essential. The vegetables would be leftovers from other meals.

Eating out – and outside – is one of the great pleasures of Provence. I have given it generous coverage in the itineraries and I

Seafood special

make a number of recommendations at the end of each section. Generally the restaurants I favour are those with menus reflecting what is seasonally and locally available. The most common regional dishes are listed in the *Menu Decoder* in this section *(see page 73)*.

Breakfast in Provence typically features a coffee and perhaps a *croissant*, *pain au chocolat* or a *brioche aux raisins*. As a rule, outside the main towns this area of the *boulanger*'s art is neglected in Provence and the pastries are often not very inspiring. If you find this to be the case, by mid-morning you will need a *casse croûte* – literally to break the crust – otherwise known as a snack. Many cafés have a menu of *casse croûte* and this is an area in which the *boulangers* of Provence excel. The *roulot saucisson* is a very distant relation of the pink sausage meat wrapped in stodgy pastry that passes for a sausage roll in England.

Pizza maker

Ideal for 'casse croûte'

Lunch in France is usually taken from noon–2pm; restaurateurs will rarely want to serve you after 1.30pm, although those in the coastal areas prove exception to this rule in summer. The best value and often the best meal is the fixed menu, including a quarter-litre of wine, which is the French working-man's lunch (the *menu fixe*). Usually it is no more than *correct* (right for the price), but occasionally there will be an excellent local speciality. This type of meal finds its apotheosis at the Bistro de Paradou in Arles.

The evening should begin at 6pm with the *apéritif*, a glass of white wine in Beaumes-de-Venise but more usually a *pastis*, a blend of aromatic plants and spices slowly macerated in alcohol and aniseed essence. Each brand is marked by its own personality: Ricard and Casanis have a taste of liquorice, Pastis 51 and Pernod tend towards aniseed. Look out also for Henri Bardouin, it has an extraordinary finesse.

One pastis and your stomach will be ideally prepared for eating, two or three and the bar will remain your habitat for the evening. The evening meal usually begins at 7pm and you will rarely be served after 9pm, particularly in the countryside. During the winter months you can be pushing your luck to start eating after 7pm.

Another day, another bottle...

I have never eaten a meal in Provence without drinking a bottle of wine – not necessarily all of it myself. I recommend that you drink the local wine. Much of the *département* of the Vaucluse is in the viticultural region of the Côte du Rhône, and has some of the most famous appellations in France: Gigondas, Châteauneuf-du-Pape, Beaumes-de-Venise (the wines from these appellations are referred to in some wine lists as the Côtes du Rhône Meridionales as opposed to the Septentrionales of the northern Rhône). Here you will be able to drink very well and relatively inexpensively. The appellations of Provence begin below Avignon and continue over a vast area of the Bouches-du-Rhône and the Var (there is also a small appellation behind Nice called Bellet). Twenty years ago good wines were difficult to find outside the small appellations of Bandol, Cassis and Palette, but nowadays they can be found all over the region. Good to great red wines in the Côteaux d'Aix-en-Provence, marvellous rosés and even some white wines in the coastal areas of the Côtes de Provence appellation. My only complaint about these wines is that they are sometimes overpriced.

Where to Eat

The restaurants below follow the regions of the main itineraries in this book, and many are mentioned in the text. Price categories are based on the how much a *menu* (typically a set three-course meal with bread and a glass of wine) will cost.

Inexpensive: *menus* up to 150FF; **moderate**: *menus* between 150FF and 300FF; **expensive**: menus above 300FF

Menu Decoder – Provençal Specialities

aïoli: garlic mayonnaise with cooked vegetables and cod.

anchoïade: a purée of anchovies, olive oil and capers.

boeuf en daube: pieces of beef cooked in olive oil with bacon, onions, garlic, with red wine.

bouillabaisse: a wide variety of fish (at least 5), boiled rapidly in olive oil with saffron.

bourride: same genre as above but with white fish and served with garlic.

grenouilles à la Provençale: frogs' legs, coated with flour and grilled in olive oil with garlic.

lapin à la Provençale: rabbit cooked slowly in white wine, with garlic, mustard, herbs and carrots.

loup au fenouil: loup grilled with fennel.

pieds-paquets: packets of tripe cooked very slowly in white wine with onions and carrots.

soupe au pistou: vegetable soup with a base of basil and garlic crushed in olive oil.

tapenade: purée of black olives and capers mixed with olive oil.

The Vaucluse

Séguret

RESTAURANT LE MESCLUN
Tel: 04 90 46 93 43
A gastronomic treat. Booking essential. Closed Mondays. Moderate.

Mt-Ventoux

LE MAS DES VIGNES
Tel: 04 90 65 63 91
This place offers good-quality local cooking and some wonderful views over the Dentelles de Montmirail. Moderate.

Gigondas

HOTELLERIE 'LES FLORETS'
Tel: 04 90 65 85 01
Located 2km (1 mile) from Gigondas in the foothills of the Dentelles. Lovely restaurant with terrace for outdoor dining. Moderate.

RESTAURANT L'OUSTALET
Tel: 04 90 65 85 30
In the centre of Gigondas. Traditional Provençal cooking, first-rate wine list. Moderate.

Beaumes-de-Venise

RESTAURANT LOU CASTELLET
Tel: 04 90 65 00 75
An ambitious restaurant where – as the French would say – the rapport between price and quality is excellent. Moderate.

Vaison-la-Romaine

LE BATELEUR
1 Place Théodore Aubanel
Tel: 04 90 36 28 04
A friendly restaurant beside the river specialising in fish dishes. Moderate.

Avignon

HIÉLY
5 Rue République.
Tel: 04 90 86 17 07
Normally closed 18 June–4 July and Monday and Tuesday – except in July. Avignon's temple of gastronomy. Famous for its classic cuisine shaped by the best regional ingredients and great wine list. Booking essential. Moderate.

LA FOURCHETTE
17 Rue Racine
Tel: 04 90 85 20 93
Atmospheric bistro-style restaurant, also run by the Hiély family. Busy at lunch time. Moderate.

LA TACHE D'ENCRE
22 Rue des Teinturiers
Tel: 04 90 86 34 84
Café-theatre with live music at weekends. Good *plat du jour* for lunch at 50FF. Teinturiers is one of the most interesting streets in Avignon and a key location for the alternative theatre during the festival. Inexpensive.

ROSE AU PETIT BEDON
(The Little Paunch)
70 Rue Joseph-Vernet
Tel: 90 82 33 98
Closed Sunday. Provençal specialities, another favourite. Inexpensive.

Châteauneuf-du-Pape

LA GARBURE
3 Rue Joseph-Ducos
Tel: 04 90 83 75 08
Centrally located with good local cuisine and accommodation in several cosy rooms. Inexpensive.

MERE GERMAINE
3 Rue Cdt Lemaitre
Tel: 04 90 83 54 37
Colourful bar and brasserie, offering splendid views and good local wines. Moderate.

Arles

BRASSERIE DE NORD-PINUS
Place du Forum
Tel: 90 93 44 44 (hotel) or
04 90 93 02 32
This place is attached to the hotel, with a dining area on the square. Stylish brasserie offering regional cuisine. Moderate.

L'AFFENAGE
4 Rue Moliere
Tel: 04 90 96 07 67
Classic Provençal dishes in friendly rustic ambience; the buffet is especially good value. Moderate.

Les Baux

OUSTAU DE BAUMANIERE
Tel: 04 90 54 33 07
This is one of the famous restaurants in France and also a luxury hotel. Superbly elegant Provençal cuisine with own grown vegetables. Expensive.

Mausanne

BISTROT DU PARADOU
Tel: 04 90 54 32 70
Tiny village bistro with a big reputation for its food, especially the vegetable *aioli*. One *menu* only. Moderate.

St-Rémy

LE RESTAURANT DES ARTS
30 Boulevard Victor Hugo
Tel: 04 90 92 08 50
Cafe, art gallery and hotel as well as a restaurant, a favourite local gathering place. Inexpensive.

JARDIN DE FRÉDÉRIC
8 Boulevard Gambetta.
Tel: 04 90 92 27 76.
Provençal menus in a sweet little auberge on main boulevard. Moderate.

Aix-en-Provence

CLOS DE LA VIOLETTE
10 Avenue de la Violette
Tel: 04 42 23 30 71
Considered the top restaurant in Aix. The chef Jean-Marc Banzo studied with Hiély in Avignon. The garden is a lovely, comfortable place to eat in the evening. Closed Sunday and Monday, also Wednesday out of season, 2 weeks in February and 2 weeks in August. Booking essential in July. Expensive.

COTÉ COUR
19 Cours Mirabeau
Tel: 04 42 93 12 51
A beautifully designed, fashionable restaurant. Classic Provençal cooking accompanied by an interesting wine list. Moderate.

Marseille

MIRAMAR
12 quai Port.
Tel: 04 91 91 10 40
A Marseille institution set right on the old port. The place to sample *bouillabaisse*. Expensive.

Make your reservations early

L'ÉPUISETTE
Vallon des Auffes.
Tel: 04 91 52 17 82
Perched high up on the rocky *calanque* of Vallon des Auffes, this restaurant offers impressive views and excellent Provençal cuisine. Moderate.

CHEZ VINCENT
25 Rue Glandeves
Tel: 04 91 33 96 78
Popular and good-value Italian restaurant located in the old port, serving great pasta and pizzas. No credit cards. Inexpensive.

A roadside stop

Special at Marseille's Miramar

Along the Coast

Cassis

RESTAURANT PANISSE
4 Place Mirabeau
Tel: 04 42 01 93 93
This place serves locally caught fish and offers delighful views over the harbour. Inexpensive.

St-Tropez

LA PESQUIERE
1 Rue des Remparts
Tel: 94 97 05 92
Excellent traditional fish dishes served. Moderate.

LA MARJOLAINE
Rue François-Sibile
Tel: 04 94 97 04 60
Typical *trattoria* cooking, offering good dishes with veal, pizza, pasta and local shrimps. Inexpensive.

LE BISTROT DES LICES
3 Place des Lices
Tel: 04 94 55 82 82
Trendy bistrot with a great ambience, good music and tasty Provençal cooking. Moderate.

LA BOUILLABAISSE
Plage de la Bouillabaisse
Tel: 04 94 97 54 00
Beach terrace restaurant for fresh salads and light pasta meals; *bouillabaisse* must be ordered a day in advance. Moderate.

The Var

Cotignac

LA FONTAINE
27 Cours Gambetta
Tel: 04 94 04 79 13

Very popular place with the locals, especially on Tuesdays (market day). Moderate.

Aups

LE YUCCA
3 Rue Foch
Tel: 04 94 70 12 11
Delightful restaurant with a flowery garden terrace. Ideal for sampling the local truffle crop. Moderate.

Villecroze-les-Grottes

AUBERGE DES LAVANDES
Place de Gaulle
Tel: 04 94 70 76 00
Country-style *auberge* (several rooms available) with good Provençal cooking on the menu. Inexpensive.

RESTAURANT LE COLOMBIER
Route de Draguignan
Tel: 04 94 70 63 23
Situated a short walk from Villecroze. Classic cooking with a regional accent. Moderate.

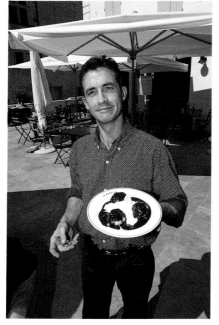

The Luberon

Roussillon

RESTAURANT LE VAL DES FÉES
Rue Richard Casteau
Tel: 04 90 05 64 99
One of the best restaurants in the Luberon, with a delightful terrace overlooking the Val de Fées. Good for special occasions. Moderate.

Gordes

RESTAURANT LE RENAISSANCE
Tel: 04 90 72 02 02
Scrumptious regional cooking. If you don't feel like driving home afterwards and want to spend the night, there are three bedrooms available. Inexpensive.

Manosque

DOMINIQUE BUCAILLE
43 Bd des Tilleuils
Tel: 04 92 72 32 38
Good-value regional dishes from a noted chef. Try the local Sisteron lamb. Moderate.

Bonnieux

LE FOURNIL
5 Place Carnot
Tel: 04 90 75 83 62
Ideal for a leisurely meal at lunch time. Shady terrace with fountain. Quality regional food. Inexpensive.

Dessert on its way

Calendar of Special Events

FEBRUARY / MARCH

Bormes-les-Mimosa
10 February: Grand Mimosa Parade.
Arles
Easter weekend: *Feria* (bullfights).

APRIL

Châteauneuf-du-Pape
24 April: Wine-growers' Festival (blessing of the vines).
Avignon
Late April, early May: Avignon Fair.

Entertainment in Arles

MAY

May Day: Festivals throughout Provence.
Arles
1 May: Feast of the Gardians (the cowboys of the Camargue).
Aups
12 May: Festival of St Pancras.
St-Tropez
16, 17, 18 May: *La Bravade,* commemorating the arrival of the beheaded Christian martyr Torpes (St Tropez) by boat in the town.
Les-Saintes-Maries-de-la-Mer
24, 25 May: popular festival and pilgrimage.

JUNE

Regionwide
24 June: Feast Day of St John the Baptist, celebrated across Provence.
Les Baux
Last Saturday in June: Folklore Festival of John the Baptist.
Tarascon
Last Sunday in June: Festival of *Tarasque,* one of Provence's best-known religious festivals.

JULY

Arles
International Festival of Photography and Festival of Arles (bullfights, music, theatre).
Avignon
Early July: Festival of French and American Cinema.
Last two weeks of July/first week of August: Festival of Theatre.
Vacqueyras
Wine Festival of local Côtes du Rhone Villages appellations.
Bastille Day
14 July: firework displays and festivals all over Provence.
Vaison-la-Romaine
Last two weeks of July: Festival of Music and Dance.
Aix-en-Provence
Last week of July: Festival of Music.
Beaumes-de-Venise
Last Sunday in July: local festival.
Cotignac
Late July–early August: Festival de la Falaise, theatre and music.
Gordes
Between the last weekend of July and the first weekend of August: Festival of Theatre and Music.

AUGUST

Ramatuelle
First two weeks of August: Festival of Theatre and Music.
La Ciotat
Festival of Cinema.
Châteauneuf-du-Pape
Wine Festival.
St-Rémy
15 August: Provençal Festival.
Séguret
Third week in August: Provençal Festival.
Apt
Last Sunday in August: Festival of St-Anne.

SEPTEMBER

Les-Saintes-Maries-de-la-Mer
1st Sunday in September: Pilgrimage.
Arles
Mid-September: Premices du Riz (the rice harvest festival).

NOVEMBER

Avignon
Mid-November: Festival of the Côtes du Rhône *primeurs* (first wines).

DECEMBER

Les Baux
Christmas Eve: La Fête du Pastrage.
Séguret
Christmas Eve: Festival of the Nativity.
Arles
Late December/early January: Salon International des Santonniers, an event that gathers together nativity scenes and *santons*.

PRACTICAL Information

GETTING THERE

By Air

Provence has two international airports, Marseille-Provence and Nice-Côte d'Azur. Marseille-Provence, less than 20km (12 miles) from both Aix and Marseille, is convenient for the places covered in this guide.

Air France (tel, UK: 0845 084 5111; US: 1-800 237 2747; www.airfrance. com) operates flights from Paris to Nice, Marseille, Avignon and Nîmes. **British Airways** (tel, UK: 0345 222 111; US: 1-800 247 9297; www. britishairways.com) flies to Nice from Heathrow and Manchester. **British Midland** (tel: 0870 607

0555; www.britishmidland.com) fly direct to Nice from Heathrow and East Midlands and via either of these two airports from Aberdeen, Belfast, Edinburgh, Glasgow, Leeds, Manchester and Teeside. Low-cost flights to Nice are operated by **Easyjet** (tel, UK: 0870 600 0000; Nice: 04 93 21 48 33; www.easyjet.com) from Luton and Liverpool and from Stansted by **GO** (tel: 0870 607 6543; www.go-fly.com). **Buzz** flies to Marseille from Stansted (tel: 0870 240 7070; www.buzzaway.com).

Both Nice-Côte d'Azur and Marseille-Provence airports operate regular buses to the main railway stations. Taxis, especially in Nice, can be expensive.

By Rail

From Paris the TGV (*train à grande vitesse*) takes 3hr 30 minutes to Avignon and 4hr 15 minutes to Marseille. A new TGV line to Marseille opening in 2001 will reduce the time to 3 hrs. Since the opening of the Channel Tunnel, travelling to Provence by rail has become an attractive option for UK visitors. Information and reservations are available from Rail Europe (179 Piccadilly, tel: 0870 5848 848 and you can book online at www.raileurope.co.uk or www.sncf.fr.

Neither Aix nor Arles are on main lines, but they are linked by local lines to Marseille and Avignon respectively.

By Car

A car is essential to make the most of Provence. However, car-hire in France is expensive (rarely less than £40 a day), so it is worth taking your own. You can do this either by ferry or on Le Shuttle (up to four trains an hour in summer), if coming from the UK.

Driving to Provence from Paris and the North involves ploughing down the *autoroute du soleil* and paying heavy tolls. If you are determined to avoid the motorways, you could follow the *itinéraires bis* (after the *bison futé* – crafty bison – whose symbol used to advertise the roads). A map of these routes can be obtained from motorway tourist offices.

Driving

You should carry in the car at all times a full driving licence, your vehicle registration document and evidence of insurance cover. You are also required to carry a red warning triangle for breakdowns and a spare set of bulbs.

Seat belts must be worn by the driver and all passengers. Full or dipped headlights must be used at night. If you have a right-hand drive vehicle it is important either to tint headlights yellow or apply special stickers that regulate the beam.

Speed Limits

Urban areas, 50kph (37mph).
Single carriageway roads, 90kph (56mph); on wet roads 80kph/50mph.
Dual carriageway roads, 110kph (68mph); on wet roads 100kph/62mph.
Motorways, 130kph (80mph); on wet roads 110kph/68mph.
Speeding offences are subject to an on-the-spot fine. Drinking and driving is also heavily penalised by on-the-spot fines.

Visas and Passports

All persons entering France must be in possession of a valid passport. Regulations vary for other countries, but most, including the US, only require a visa after 3 months. They can be obtained for a nominal fee from any French consulate.

When to Visit

Statistics show that Provence has 2,500–2,800 hours of sun each year. There are clear, sunny days at all times of the year. Sun and heat are virtually guaranteed in July and August. There is a marked change at the end of August, when a few spectacular thunderstorms race through the region and the mistral is more likely to blow. As a result, the light has a special brilliancy in September and October.

I have the impression that the mistral, the famous wind of Provence, is less in evidence than it was. Referred to in Provençal mythology as *le maître* (the master), it is said to blow 170 days a year in some areas of Provence. Technically the wind is born in the plain of Valence where cold air from the mountains is attracted by huge masses of warm air over the Mediterranean. It starts with particular gusto when a depression of warm air comes up from the southern Mediterranean. Bottled into a narrow corridor, the wind accelerates rapidly and is uncorked in the Bouches-du-Rhône, its effects felt all over the Vaucluse and the Var.

The months of November and December are likely to be fairly wet, but around Christmas time the weather is often beautifully clear, and you can often eat outside at midday (nights, however, are cold). The temperature climbs from the end of March but the weather will be variable until the end of June – periods of very warm weather, interspersed with those of unsettled weather.

The itineraries in this book are geared to the summer months of July and August, when Provence is *en fête*, animated by innumerable festivals. This is, however, also when it is particularly crowded by the coast.

Clothing

Take cool, comfortable, casual clothes in summer. Don't forget a sun hat, sunglasses and sun cream, and a sweater for the evening. At other times of year dress as you would for any temperate climate.

Electricity

France runs on 220V, with double, round-pin sockets. A socket adaptor is required for the British 3-pin plug. A voltage transformer will be required for electrical goods that originated in countries, such as the USA, where the current alternates at 60 cycles and not the European standard of 50 cycles.

Time

France is one hour ahead of GMT, 6 and 9 hours respectively ahead of the US time zones (Eastern Standard Time and Pacific Standard Time).

MONEY MATTERS

Banks

Opening hours: Monday–Friday, 9am–noon, 2–4.30pm.

Currency

The units of the currency in France are currently francs and centimes. Denominations: notes, 500FF, 200FF, 100FF, 50FF and 20FF; coins, 10FF, 5FF, 2FF, 1FF; and 50, 20, 10 and 5 centime pieces. Many shops and businesses now indicate prices in both francs and euros, and euro coins and notes will be introduced in January 2002. Francs will be accepted until June 30 2002.

Credit Cards

Credit cards have a wide but by no means universal currency in Provence. The 'market' economy is still lubricated by cash. Many wine producers and restaurants do not accept cards. Traveller's cheques are useful. Eurocheques are no longer accepted.

Cash Machines

In theory PIN numbers are universally recognised, though sometimes French machines fail to recognise the magnetic strips on foreign cards. The majority of cash machines in France accept Visa, Maestro and Cirrus.

Tipping

This is included in the bill in restaurants, hotels and cafés. Exceptional service can be rewarded with a tip, the *pourboire* (literally meaning, 'for a drink'). Hairdressers, taxi drivers, porters and doormen will all expect a small tip.

HOLIDAYS & HOURS

Business Hours

The lunch break remains sacrosanct throughout Provence and in many villages noon is even announced by a siren. Banks, tourist offices, museums, shops, petrol stations, post offices – almost everything, in fact – will close for two hours.

The basic working hours are 9am–noon and 2–6pm, although supermarkets and other shops staying open until 7.30 or 8pm do not generally reopen until 3.30pm.

The working week is usually Tuesday–Saturday; even quite large towns can be deserted on a Monday.

Public Holidays

There are 12 *jours fériés*, or public holidays in France. These are:
1 January
Easter Monday
1 May
8 May (V-E Day)
Ascension Thursday
Whit Monday (the Monday following the seventh Sunday after Easter)
14 July (Bastille Day)
15 August (Assumption)
1 November (All Saints' Day)
11 November (Armistice Day 1918)
Christmas Day
26 December

Closed for lunch?

Hotel Crillon Le Brave

ACCOMMODATION
Hotels

The local Tourist Office *(see page 91)* can be a very useful resource if you have trouble finding accommodation. Tourist Offices will have lists of *gîtes*, self-catering holiday cottages, rentable for just a weekend or for periods up to several weeks, *chambres d'hôtes* (the French equivalent of bed and breakfast), and camping sites – which are very often superbly equipped.

The following list of recommendations is structured so that it follows the main sections of this guide. Price indications given are based on single occupancy:
Budget: under 200FF
Moderate: 200FF–600FF
Expensive: over 600FF

Breakfast is not included in the price of a room.

Vaucluse
Bédoin

HOTEL CRILLON LE BRAVE
Tel: 04 90 65 61 61
Situated in a stunning location opposite Mt-Ventoux with lovely gardens, a good restaurant and superb rooms in Provençal style. Expensive.

HOTEL RESTAURANT L'ESCAPADE
Tel: 04 90 65 60 21
Has a good restaurant that is great value. Look out for the *menu du jour*. Budget.

HOTEL DES PINS
Chemin des Crans
Tel: 04 90 65 92 92
Delightful hotel with lovely views and a swimming pool. Moderate.

Vaison-la-Romaine

HOTEL LE BEFFROI
Tel: 04 90 36 04 71
A characterful hotel situated in the *haute ville*. As well as offering a good restaurant, it has a 17th-century *salon* with original beamed ceiling and fireplace. Moderate.

HOTEL BURRHUS
Tel: 04 90 36 00 11
Provençal-style townhouse located in the lively Place Montfort. Moderate.

Seguret

HOTEL RESTAURANT LA TABLE DU COMTAT
Tel: 04 90 46 91 49
Small and intimate, with just eight bedrooms. Superb restaurant and a perfect setting. Expensive.

La Table du Comta

Avignon

HOTEL EUROPE
12 Place Crillon.
Tel: 04 90 14 76 76
The Europe is probably Avignon's best hotel. Once a coaching inn, mentioned in many early travellers' accounts. Favoured by celebrity types. Conveniently situated, very quiet, elegant and comfortable. Expensive.

HOTEL MIGNON
12 Rue Joseph-Vernet
Tel: 04 90 82 17 30
Mignon means cute or sweet in French, and it is. Budget.

MERCURE PALAIS DES PAPES
Quartier Balance
Tel: 04 90 85 91 23
Centrally located convenient, modern, Provençal-style hotel. Expensive.

REGINA HOTEL
6 Rue de la République
Tel: 04 90 86 49 45
Just off the Place de l'Horloge, a nicely modernised hotel and quite a bargain for the centre of Avignon. Moderate.

HOTEL SAINT-GEORGE
12 Traverse de l'Etoile
Tel: 04 90 88 54 34
Outside the ramparts on the road to Marseille. Clean, friendly and good value. Budget.

Collias

HOSTELLERIE LE CASTELLAS
Tel: 04 66 22 88 88
A converted 17th-century governor's mansion, where it is a delight to stay. Moderate.

Arles

GRAND HOTEL NORD-PINUS
Place du Forum
Tel: 04 90 93 44 44
Insight Guides' top recommendation in Arles. This is a luxury hotel redolent with the history and culture of Arles, particularly when its superb bar 'La Corrida' is packed with matadors and their flamboyant retinues. Great Art Deco brasserie. Expensive.

HOTEL D'ARLATEN
26 Rue du Sauvage
Tel: 04 90 93 56 66
The beautifully restored home of the Counts of Arlaten, just off Place du Forum. Moderate.

Hotel du Forum

HOTEL CALENDAL
22 Place Pomme
Tel: 04 90 96 11 89
Offers good rooms and a shady garden in a convenient location behind the Arena. Moderate.

HOTEL LE CLOITRE
16 Rue du Cloître
Tel: 04 90 96 29 50
Quiet Provençal-style hotel in a narrow street behind the Cloisters. Moderate.

HOTEL DU FORUM
Place du Forum
Tel: 04 90 93 48 95
Lacks the style of the Nord-Pinus but a comfortable hotel with the great advantage of a swimming pool in a secluded courtyard. Moderate.

HOTEL DE MUSÉE
11 Rue du Grand Prieuré
Tel: 04 90 93 88 88
A 17th-century mansion tucked away on a winding street, with a pretty courtyard for breakfast. Moderate.

St Rémy

HOTEL DES ANTIQUES
15 Avenue Pasteur
Tel: 04 90 92 03 02
Fin de siècle charm, lovely garden – you could call it a park – and pool. Moderate.

MAS DES CARASSINS
1 Chemin Gaulois
Tel: 04 90 92 15 48
This is a converted farmhouse set in secluded gardens just outside St Remy. Moderate.

Aix-en-Provence

HOTEL DES AUGUSTINS
3 Rue de la Masse
Tel: 04 42 27 28 59
Impressive hotel in an old religious house. Two of the rooms have private terraces. Expensive.

GRAND HOTEL NEGRE COSTE
33 Cours Mirabeau
Tel: 04 42 27 74 22
Magnificent old hotel set on Aix's elegant main street. Fine views. Moderate.

LE MANOIR
8 Rue d'Entrecasteaux
Tel: 04 42 26 27 20
Comfortable old-style hotel, breakfast in the 14th-century cloister. Moderate.

LE PIGONNET
5 Avenue du Pigonnet
Tel: 04 42 59 02 90
Luxurious old country house-hotel, in a park in the middle of Aix. Expensive.

HOTEL DES QUATRE DAUPHINS
54 Rue Roux Alphéran
Tel: 04 42 38 16 39
In the Mazarin quarter, near the fountain of the same name. Cramped but convenient. Moderate.

Along the Coast
Cassis

HOTEL-RESTAURANT LE JARDIN D'EMILE
23 Avenue Amiral Ganteaume
Tel: 04 42 01 80 55
Located in a gorgeous tropical garden on Plage du Bestouan. Great restaurant. Moderate.

Cassis also has a good campsite, around 10-minutes' walk from the sea: Les Cigales, Route de Marseille; tel: 04 42 01 07 34.

Bormes-les-Mimosas

LE GRAND HOTEL
167 Route de Baguier
Tel: 04 94 71 23 72
Old-style hotel in a garden of palms overlooking the village. Moderate.

MIRAGE
38 Rue de la Vue des Iles
Tel: 04 94 05 32 60

Elegant hotel with a pool and great views out to the islands. Expensive.

Iles d'Hyeres/Porquerolles

LES GLYCINES
Place d'Armes
Tel: 04 94 58 30 36
Delightful Provençal-style hotel with a good-value restaurant. Moderate.

Gassin

HOTEL RESTAURANT BELLO VISTO
Place des Barrys
Tel: 04 94 56 17 30
A lovely hotel with a good restaurant. Just one of a number of similar establishments on the *Place des Barrys,* with terraces looking towards the bay of Pampelonne. Moderate.

St-Tropez

Recommending hotels in St-Tropez is easy; finding a room if you have not booked well in advance is difficult, probably impossible in the summer.

LOU CAGNARD
18 Avenue P Roussel
Tel: 94 97 04 24
This place is in a more peaceful position than the others, towards the rear of the town and behind the Place des Lices. Closed November–December. Moderate.

HOTEL DE LA PONCHE
3 Rue des Remparts
Tel: 04 94 97 02 53
This hotel is formed from a number of old fishermen's cottages. Exquisitely furnished. Closed from 15 October–1 April. Expensive.

LE PRE DE LA MER
Route des Salins
Tel: 04 94 97 12 23
Pretty Provençal hotel with self-contained apartments, just outside town. Expensive.

The Var
Salernes

HOTEL ALLEGRE
20 Rue J. J. Rousseau
Tel: 04 94 70 60 30
Everything about this hotel is *correct* (just right) and unchanging. The hotel's restaurant has a good reputation in the surrounding area. Moderate.

Cotignac

HOSTELLERIE LOU CALEN
1 Cours Gambetta
Tel: 04 94 04 60 40
This is one of the best hotels in the area, with a shady garden and a large swimming pool. The restaurant also has a good reputation. Moderate.

RESTAURANT HOTEL DU COURS
18 Cours Gambetta
Tel: 04 94 04 78 50
A good bargain hotel with *pension complet.* The restaurant has a good value menu including wine. Budget.

Aups

AUBERGE DE LA TOUR
Rue Eglise
Tel: 04 94 70 00 30
Probably the smartest spot in the town. The restaurant does good pizzas. Moderate.

GRAND HOTEL
Place Gendarme-Duchatel
Tel: 04 94 70 10 82
Friendly, *correct* hotel with a good restaurant. Moderate.

LE PROVENÇAL
Place Bidouret
Tel: 04 94 70 00 24
Small, rustic hotel. Budget.

Tourtour

BASTIDE DE TOURTOUR
Tel: 04 98 10 54 20

Luxury hotel in its own park with pool and restaurant. Expensive.

LA PETITE AUBERGE
1km (½ mile) south of the village on the D77
Tel: 04 94 70 57 16
Imagine having the view that you see from the orientation point from your own bedroom. Add a swimming pool and a good restaurant and you have something special – La Petite Auberge. Moderate.

The Luberon
Apt

AUBERGE DU LUBERON
17 Quai Léon-Sagy
Tel: 04 90 74 12 50
The best hotel in Apt, just across the river from the Place de la Bouquerie. Good restaurant. Moderate.

HOTEL LE PALAIS
Place Gabriel Péri
Tel: 04 90 04 89 32
Good cheap rooms in the middle of town. Budget.

Roussillon

HOTEL 'RÉSIDENCE DES OCRES'
Route de Gordes
Tel: 04 90 05 60 50
Set in the heart of the village, with air-conditioned rooms. Moderate.

Gordes

LA BASTIDE DE GORDES
Route de Combe
Tel: 04 90 72 12 12
Smart hotel on the town walls with splendid views of surrounding country. Expensive.

LES BORIES
On the D177 to Sénanque
Tel: 04 90 72 00 51
This place began life as a rustic hostel in a few *bories (see page 62)*. It is still talked of in those terms but, make no mistake, this is now a luxury hotel. Fixed price lunch. Expensive.

AUBERGE DE CARCARILLE
2km east of Gordes on the D2
Tel: 04 90 72 02 63
The Auberge de Carcarille, which has its own swimming pool, is set in the countryside, so you'll probably need a car to get here. The restaurant is considered to be good for the price. Moderate.

Bonnieux

HOTEL CÉSAR
Place de la Liberté
Tel: 04 90 75 96 35
The dining room at this hotel looks out over the valley to Lacoste, which is delightful. Moderate.

NIGHTLIFE

Come meet me in some dead café –
A puff of cognac or a sip of smoke.
(from *Avignon* by Lawrence Durrell)

Nightlife in Provence is sitting in the Place du Forum in Arles listening to a saxophone and bass improvise around the chords of *Round Midnight;* it is ordering just one last bottle of rosé with the patron yawning; it is the village ball and *fête*. It might be drinking a coffee or promenading on the Cours Mirabeau, or listening to the string quartet on the terrace of a château. It is occasionally an open-air film, the festival of theatre in Avignon, classical music in Aix or jazz in Hyères. It can be the nightclub, but that is really the preserve of the coast and above all St-Tropez, and it disappears completely in winter.

The best guides to what is on are the local papers and a listings magazine, published on Wednesday, called *La Semaine des Spectacles*.

Nightlife coming to the Place du Forum, Arles

HEALTH & EMERGENCIES

The number for the emergency services is 15.

France has one of the best national health services in the world. However, the patient has to pay many of the costs up front and 75–80 percent of these are later reimbursed. The advantage for the visitor of this system is that there is little bureaucracy involved; doctors and hospitals will treat everyone without worrying about whether a patient is a member of their scheme or health authority.

Citizens of the EC are entitled to health care in France on the same terms as the French; that is, payment and reimbursement by their own government. British citizens will find that this process is smoother if the doctor or hospital giving treatment fills out form E111 (obtainable in Britain before you leave).

Refunds extend to any medicines prescribed by the doctor. Be warned, however: doctors in France prescribe very freely and the pharmacies, though excellent, are rather expensive. They are one of the last cartels, enjoying a monopoly of the sale of all medicines, even aspirins. One point in their favour is that a pharmacist has considerable powers to prescribe medicine. For minor problems consult a pharmacist before visiting a doctor.

As in any country, it is always advisable to take out your own private medical insurance before travelling.

Police and Crime

The number for an emergency is 17.

Petty theft is inevitably a problem in the bigger towns and on the coast, although less so in rural areas. Tape decks and luggage in cars are the usual targets. Thefts should be reported to the local *gendarmerie* (police station), where you will be issued with the necessary papers to make an insurance claim. A tip: don't go at lunch time.

Fires

The number for an emergency is 18.

Forest fires are a perennial problem in Provence, and fire fighting equipment is in place in every *commune*. Devastation every year is severe; the heavily forested department of the Var suffers most.

Cooking on an open fire in the forest and while *camping sauvage* (outside designated sites) are both forbidden in Provence, and infringements are

Guardians of the law in Aix

heavily penalised. You should be very careful with cigarette ends, etc.

POST

Most post offices open from 9am–noon and 2–5pm, Monday to Friday and 9am–noon on Saturday. Stamps *(timbres)* can also be bought from *tabacs*, which can be found in many bars.

TELEPHONES

Telephone numbers in France are now in ten figures, which are always written in sets of two, e.g. 04 23 45 67 89 (04 is the code for Provence). To telephone France from abroad, omit the initial zero. The cheapest times to telephone are weekdays 7pm to 8am and at weekends.

International calls

To make an international call from Provence, dial 00 followed by the country's international call number. These can be found in the front of the *Pages Jaunes* section of the telephone directory *(annuaire)* or on the information section in a telephone box.

Australia 00 61
Canada 00 1
Ireland 00 353
New Zealand 00 64
South Africa 00 27
UK 00 44
US 00 1
Monaco 00 377

If using a US credit phone card, call the company's access number: AT&T, 0800-99-00-11; MCI, 0800-99-00-19; Sprint, 0800-99-0087.

Public Phones

Coin-operated phones take most coins and card phones are now very common. Cards are available from post offices, stationers, railway stations, some cafés and bureaux de tabacs.

MEDIA

Regional and provincial papers account for over two-thirds of the daily sale, a pattern similar to the US. Newspapers such as *Le Provençal* and *Var Matin* have only a few pages of hard news but are excellent sources of local information of all kinds.

INFORMATION & MAPS

The itineraries in this guide have been traced on the pull-out map in the wallet at the back of this guide. Other good maps of the region include Michelin map No. 245, in the series 1cm: 2km (coloured yellow), or map No 115 in the *Institut Géographique National* red series, 1cm: 2½km.

Local tourist offices are good sources for town plans and local maps, and for information regarding opening hours of museums and other local attractions, as well as restaurants.

In the Vaucluse such tourist offices are very strong on publicising outdoor activities and they will usually supply maps specifically designed for walkers and cyclists.

LANGUAGE

The curiosity of the French language in Provence is the accent. Many words finish with a kind of clanging sound. The most important thing to remember is that *rapports sociale* are more formal in France than in many countries – witness the shaking of hands and the ritual of the *bise* (kiss).

The following are useful phrases:

Good morning/hello	*Bonjour*
Good evening	*Bonsoir*
How are you?	*Comment allez-vous?*
I'm well	*Très bien, merci*
Goodbye	*Au revoir*
Please	*S'il vous plaît*
Yes please	*S'il vous plaît*
Thank you	*Merci*
You are welcome	*Je vous en prie*
Enjoy your meal	*Bon appetit*
See you later	*A tout à l'heure*

USEFUL ADDRESSES

Tourist Offices

Aix-en-Provence: Place de Général de Gaulle, 13100 Aix-en-Provence. Tel: 04 42 16 11 61.
Apt: 20 Ave Philippe de Gerard, 84400 Apt. Tel: 04 90 74 03 18.

Arles: Esplanade Charles de Gaulle, 13200 Arles. Tel: 04 90 18 41 20.
Avignon: 41 Cours Jean Jaurès, 84000 Avignon. Tel: 04 32 74 32 74.
Aups: Place Mairie, 83630 Aups. Tel: 04 94 70 00 80.
Cassis: Place P. Baragnon, 13260 Cassis. Tel: 04 42 01 71 17.
Salernes: Rue Victor Hugo, 83690 Salernes. Tel: 04 94 70 69 02.
St Tropez: Quai Jean Jaures, 83990 St-Tropez. Tel: 04 94 97 45 21.
Vaison-la-Romaine: Place du Chanoine Sautel, 84110 Vaison. Tel: 04 90 36 02 11.
London: French Tourist Office, 178 Piccadilly, London W1V 9DB. Tel: 09068 244123. www.franceguide.com
New York: French Tourist Office, 444 Madison Avenue, New York, NY 10022. Tel: 212 838 7800.

FURTHER READING

Travels Through France and Italy by Tobias Smollett, The World's Classics, Oxford University Press, 1990.
Hills and the Sea by Hilaire Belloc, Methuen & Co, 1906.
Letters from My Windmill by Alphonse Daudet, Penguin.
Collected Stories by Colette, Penguin.
Petrarch and his World by Morris Bishop, Chatto & Windus.
The Waning of the Middle Ages by J Huizinga, Penguin (classic study, good on the Courts of Love).
Provence by Ford Madox Ford, Allen & Unwin.
The Wines of the Rhône Valley and Provence by R. Parker, Dorling Kindersley

Also by APA Publications

Insight Guide: Provence
Insight Guide: French Riviera
Insight Pocket Guide: French Riviera
Insight Compact Guide: Provence
Insight Compact Guide: French Riviera

ACKNOWLEDGMENTS

Photography **Gil Galvin and George Taylor** *and*
Page 1 **Bill Wassman**
Pages 8/9, 36B, 43, 79 **Catherine Karnow**
Production Editor **Erich Meyer**
Cover Design **Tanvir Virdee**
Cover Photography **Pictures Colour Library** *(front)*
Gil Galvin and George Taylor *(back)*
Cartography **Berndtson & Berndtson**

INSIGHT
Pocket Guides

The travel guides that replace a tour guide – now better than ever with more listings and a fresh new design

Insight Pocket Guides pioneered a new approach to guidebooks, introducing the concept of the authors as "local hosts" who would provide readers with personal recommendations, just as they would give honest advice to a friend who came to stay. They also included a full-size pull-out map. Now, to cope with the needs of the 21st century, new editions in this growing series are being given a new look to make them more practical to use, and restaurant and hotel listings have been greatly expanded.

The world's largest collection of visual travel guides

Now in association with